More Praise for *Anxiety at Work*

"Few things can paralyze the progress of any team or organization like anxiety. After decades of working with CEOs and business owners, I've noticed many have a negative mind-set when it comes to dealing with stress—a mindset that needs to be changed. *Anxiety at Work* offers practical ideas to help leaders develop healthier mindsets and healthier teams. This is a smartly written, step-by-step guide to creating a work culture that will attract and retain great people."

—*John C. Maxwell, #1* New York Times *bestselling author and world-renowned leadership expert*

"I've personally known anxiety—the struggle just to get out of bed every morning. Overcoming these feelings in myself, and helping others face their challenges, has been my life's work for the past decade. I'm so grateful Gostick and Elton have turned their attention to helping in the working world, where tens of millions of employees feel overwhelmed and overanxious. In this fabulous new book, leaders will learn how to identify anxiety in their team members, understand the triggers of anxiety, and provide the right support. *Anxiety at Work* is the tool that businesses have been waiting for."

—*Mel Robbins, daytime talk show host, CNN on-air analyst, and #1 bestselling author of* The 5 Second Rule

"When our team members feel too much anxiety, they attack change; they become combative or controlling as they try to ease the pain they feel. This makes organizational change difficult, even impossible. In this brilliant new book, Gostick and Elton help leaders build resilience with practical tools culled from decades coaching leaders to improve their organizational cultures."

—*Dr. Marshall Goldsmith, world's #1 leadership thinker and author of* What Got You Here Won't Get You There

"*Anxiety at Work* is brimming with practical ideas on how to create a safe, productive place to work—from the globally recognized thought-leaders in culture and employee engagement. This desperately needed guide will become an instant classic."

—*Dr. Tasha Eurich*, New York Times *bestselling author of* Insight *and* Bankable Leadership

"Savoring this book feels like snuggling up in a warm comforter on a cold day. The enormous demands of our world are mitigated by using the insights offered. The ideas, stories, and tools will help anyone tame apprehensions and turn anxiety into assurance."

—*Dr. Dave Ulrich, Rensis Likert Collegiate Professor, Ross School of Business, University of Michigan; partner, The RBL Group*

"Gostick and Elton have a powerful ability to tap into the true essence of workplace stress and team dysfunction, and, most important, offer up practical solutions that will help move any organization to a healthy, productive place and effect positive change."

—*Chris Rainey, host,* HR Leaders *podcast, the #1 HR podcast in the world*

"*Anxiety at Work* offers leaders a simple yet powerful approach to increase productivity and resilience by building a more compassionate workplace. When we focus on compassion, our teams are more effective, and we benefit from increased productivity and mental and physical health. In this guide, leadership experts Gostick and Elton provide the tools to help teams avoid burnout and create a single-minded focus on purpose and goals."

—*Leah Weiss, PhD, founding faculty of Stanford University's Compassion Cultivation Training program and author of* How We Work

"The best leaders harness the collective intelligence of their teams to find answers in the hardest of times. *Anxiety at Work* is a blueprint for reducing stress, building resilience, and creating an environment where people feel safe to take risks and grow. In a time of great uncertainty, this book is going to help leaders see the world in a new way and bring out the best in everyone on their team."

—*Liz Wiseman,* New York Times *bestselling author of* Multipliers *and* Rookie Smarts

"This book can change teams and lives. Absolutely an essential text for our times, inspiring and immediately useful. My greatest wonder is why it's taken so long for someone to tackle this vital topic of anxiety at work."

—*Natalie Baumgartner, PhD, chief workforce scientist, Achievers*

"*Anxiety at Work* provides an incredibly practical guide to help us lead in a world that is becoming increasingly anxiogenic and is stressing out so many. Adrian Gostick and Chester Elton's book is a very timely and generous gift to the world and will help countless leaders navigate these waters, relieve much of the stress, and enable many to live a happier, more productive life."

—*Hubert Joly, former chairman and CEO, Best Buy; author of* The Heart of Business: Leadership Principles for the Next Era of Capitalism

Also by Adrian Gostick and Chester Elton

Leading with Gratitude

The Carrot Principle

The Best Team Wins

The Orange Revolution

What Motivates Me

All In

Managing with Carrots

Anxiety at Work

8 Strategies to Help Teams Build
Resilience, Handle Uncertainty,
and Get Stuff Done

**Adrian Gostick and Chester Elton
with Anthony Gostick**

HARPER
BUSINESS

An Imprint of HarperCollins*Publishers*

HarperCollins books may be purchased for educational, business, or sales promotional use. For information, please email the Special Markets Department at SPsales@harpercollins.com.

FIRST EDITION

Library of Congress Cataloging-in-Publication Data has been applied for.

ISBN 978-0-06-304615-3

21 22 23 24 25 LSC 10 9 8 7 6 5 4 3 2 1

To Anthony Gostick

This book is dedicated to one of its authors by the other two. Without Anthony, this book would not exist. His research and writing were foundational, but it was his never-ending passion for positive mental health that inspired us to create something that we hope will make the world a better place.

Contents

Anxiety
at
Work

The Duck Syndrome

CREATING A HEALTHY
PLACE TO WORK

—

It is not the strongest of the species that survives, nor the most intelligent, it is the one most adaptable to change.

—Charles Darwin (paraphrased by Leon Megginson)

In early 2020, we were in Scottsdale, Arizona, to give a speech to the leadership team of a manufacturing company. We'd originally been scheduled to address the group at the end of the day, but the organizers kept moving our start time up. They wanted to end the day early because of the flood of fast-breaking news about the spread of the coronavirus.

Concentrating on the event proceedings was nearly impossible for the attendees with everyone constantly checking their phones for the latest news and texts from loved ones. Employees at the company's factories were asking if they should go home. Within a few days, hand sanitizer and toilet paper would inexplicably disappear from shelves, and within weeks, tens of thousands of people would be sick.

In the back of the ballroom we were huddled over our presentation, frantically changing it in real time. The material we'd been asked to share on culture and employee engagement didn't seem nearly as relevant anymore. We decided we would instead unveil research we'd been compiling about the growing problem of workplace anxiety, which was going to be even more urgent heading into a period of great uncertainty. It was clear that many jobs would be lost in the fallout of COVID-19, and those who kept their positions would be under great pressure. Data we were about to present would show that levels of anxiety at work had been steadily rising well before this; and we predicted that things were about to get a lot worse.

When we stepped onto the stage, at least half the audience members had their heads in their phones, yet by the end of our hour together, all of us were fully engaged in a discussion about the real issues that were happening right then to their people. These leaders grasped that they needed to be more informed about the nature of anxiety and how they could best help their team members cope.

In the airport that night, after scrubbing our seats with the Clorox wipes we'd been lucky to score, we talked about the important role managers play in employees' lives. We were gratified that many leaders had already shared with us keen insights about how they'd assisted anxiety-ridden employees in our research for this book. We noted that if anxiety levels had been rising before this pandemic, we could only imagine what was going to happen now.

A Growing Issue

For some time, we have been concerned about the increasing problem of workplace anxiety and the need to provide managers realistic and useful guidance. We began researching and writing this book because in most companies we worked with, we were hearing mounting frustration and bewilderment of leaders about this issue. Research told us they had good reason to be concerned long before the pandemic. In a 2018 survey, 34 percent of workers of all ages reported feeling anxiety at least once in the previous month, and 18 percent had a diagnosed anxiety disorder. And yet very little about the problem was being talked about in their companies, despite a significant economic impact.

Harvard Medical School research claimed on-the-job anxiety "imperils workers' careers and company productivity." Anxiety is leading to increased employee errors, growing burnout, workplace rage, more sick days, and poor employee health. Concerned? Us, too. Worry, stress, and resulting anxiety at work can cause employees to lose focus and withdraw, working at a reduced capacity and rebuffing attempts by fellow team members or managers to help.

As a quick education, people sometimes use the terms "worry," "stress," and "anxiety" interchangeably. While they may travel together, they are different. Worry is a mental process—including repetitive, nagging thoughts—usually focused on a specific target like losing a job or wondering if you'll get sick. Stress is a biological reaction when changes occur, to which the body responds physically, mentally, or emotionally. Anxiety involves the body and mind and can be serious enough to qualify as a mental disorder. Anxiety can combine stress, fear, and worry in ways that interfere with life.

There are two ways to refer to anxiety: the first is as a symptom of stress and worry; the second is as a classifiable disorder. As you might imagine, the effects of a rising tide of worry, stress, and anxiety have been incredibly expensive for organizations. In America, workplace anxiety is estimated to cost some $40 billion a year in lost productivity, errors, and health-care costs, while stress is estimated to cost more than $300 billion. The Organization for Economic Co-operation and Development in Paris offers an even more dour assessment of the effects in Europe, estimating the total costs of mental health problems at more than 600 billion euros annually, with anxiety being the most common issue.

Though the problem is becoming more serious with older employees, it's been particularly acute with millennials and Gen Z. According to a 2019 study published in the *Harvard Business Review*, more than half of millennials and 75 percent of Gen Z reported they had quit a job for mental health reasons. In our consulting work, we've found that one of the greatest concerns among managers today is how to motivate younger workers. One leadership workshop Adrian conducted with a group of executives had especially driven home the problem. In the Q&A session, every one of their questions was about their younger workers—specifically about how they were having a hard time handling the pressures of their deadline-oriented business. One leader summed up the general concern for all: "How do we get our young employees to cope better? I mean, we can't stop delivering."

A big part of the problem is employee anxiety, which can present as an overestimation of workplace threats (from personal issues such as "Will I fit in?" to organizational issues that may affect the stability of the company) and an underestimation of one's ability to cope. Yet sometimes anxiety is a general state of unease for no apparent reason. As Gen Z is now flooding into the workforce, a tidal wave of anxious young people are on their way to our businesses, says Michael Fenlon, chief people officer for PricewaterhouseCoopers, one of the nation's biggest employers of newly minted college grads.

We've found most young people *want* to be able to discuss their anxiety at work. Said one twenty-something employee in an interview, "My generation talks about anxiety *all the time* to each other." Rightly so, they believe that it's impossible to fix something we are scared to talk about. And yet in a 2019 survey of one thousand employed adults with anxiety, 90 percent judged it would be a bad idea to confide their situation to their bosses. Sad.

The profound realization from the pandemic is that our world is subject to destabilizing, long-lasting threats, which may arise seemingly out of nowhere and disrupt not only companies but the whole economy. That is affecting anxiety levels like nothing we've seen before. According to the U.S. Census Bureau, by May of 2020 more than 30 percent of all Americans of all ages were reporting symptoms of an anxiety disorder, including a remarkable 42 percent of people in their twenties.

Lenny Mendonca is a prominent business owner and public official who in mid-2020 resigned from office after being hit by strains on his mental health. "I face a challenge one of every three people in America has: depression and anxiety," he said.

Mendonca had been chief economic and business advisor to California governor Gavin Newsom, and is owner of Half Moon Bay Brewing Company, which employs about four hundred people. He's also a former senior executive of McKinsey & Company and a lecturer at the Stanford Graduate School of Business. In other words, the guy is a mover and shaker.

He explained that well-meaning friends discouraged him from sharing his diagnosis, suggesting it would end his career. "While I respect their counsel, I categorically reject it. I talk about my mountain biking injuries and the metal plate in my left leg as a badge of honor. Why should I hide a similar injury to the most important—and yet vulnerable and least understood—organ in my body, my brain? What does it say about me that I have a mental health issue? It says that I am human."

Mendonca shared his story because he believes there are

too few in business and public life willing to "discuss mental health, destigmatize professional shame, and protect against the resulting economic impact it can have on people's careers and our economy as a whole. The conversation is overdue and urgent," he said.

The Cover-Up

Mendonca admits, "I have executive seniority that reduces the potential professional harm of speaking out. The majority of people suffering do not have these privileges." He's right—despite its prevalence, employees just don't talk openly about their anxiety at work. The biggest challenge—one that makes it tricky to help employees—is that many with anxiety must cover it up, which all too often ends badly.

Consider the case of a promising young employee we met in 2019.

Chloe is the kind of worker most companies are avidly recruiting: smart and personable, comfortable with technology, and an uber-fast learner. She had graduated from college with a near-perfect GPA but admitted that keeping up with the work was a challenge. She would wake up early to get in extra study time before class and most nights had trouble getting to sleep, usually managing only a few hours. Sometimes seized with anxiety from the pressure of all she had to get through, she would slap a smile on her face and keep moving, because, as she said, "that's what you're supposed to do."

Secretly she had wondered why she had to try so hard to

appear chipper when everyone else seemed to be that way naturally.

All of Chloe's hard work paid off when, after graduation, she landed a good job at an investment bank in Seattle. She moved there from her hometown across the country and quickly impressed her boss and colleagues. They considered her a surefire rising star. Outwardly, Chloe oozed confidence.

But inside, she felt out of her element. She began to doubt herself. Her young peers at the bank seemed to have more experience. Most had gone to more prestigious schools. They talked about their amazing internships. They seemed to get more recognition. "Every morning, the company sent out this mass email about someone else's accomplishments," she recalls. "It was this nice thing from HR, but to me it felt like taunting. Everyone around me was so smart, doing such cool things. I wanted to be just as wonderful as they were."

What's more, judging by social media posts, her friends back home seemed much happier than she was. They were going to parties and concerts, hanging with family, relaxing, and having fun. As for Chloe, she worked every day past dark, went back to her apartment, and crashed. She didn't even have time for a cat.

Chloe gathered her courage and mentioned to her manager that she was feeling a little overwhelmed. The manager's response: "Ah, that's what it's like around here. You're doing fine. Try not to stress." She resigned herself to feeling this way because that was just how things were. But soon, every night, Chloe felt a looming dread about the next day. Sunday evenings were the absolute worst, when she would exhibit all the signs of a full-blown panic attack. Before long she could hardly get out of bed. At work, she began scrolling through the web pages of graduate schools. She daydreamed about travel. Maybe she'd take a year off and backpack through places like Nepal.

Even though she'd put in a lot of work and had been doing well in her job, one day Chloe simply had too much. She "ghosted." She didn't show up at work and didn't call in sick. When her boss sent a text to ask where she was, she ignored it.

Chloe never went back, and she never even communicated with her manager or anyone else at the company again. A star in the making just blinked out.

From her manager's standpoint, we can imagine this was incredibly frustrating. No glaring need had been shown for any special treatment, right? How could Chloe's leader have possibly seen any signs that she was about to bolt? As you'll see, sometimes the slightest of clues can mean a lot. Chloe had admitted she was overwhelmed, and she wanted reassurance that her manager cared. But when her boss brushed off her reality, it closed off all potential to reconcile the issue.

Chloe put her toes in the water by saying she was overwhelmed and found that it wasn't really safe to talk about her anxiety at work.

Ducks at Stanford

While Chloe burned out fairly quickly, many others wrestle with intense feelings for years, becoming adept at hiding the signs. Despite a great deal of coverage in the media about rising anxiety levels, the stigma at work remains potent. Most people aren't willing to discuss what they're going through with anyone but their closest family and friends, and often not even with them.

Of course, talking about work overload is common enough: *Can you believe how much they want me to get done?!* But work overload is distinct from anxiety overload. Revealing that your job is causing you anxiety is still largely taboo, especially in an environment where employees are worried about keeping their positions. Some told us that speaking up about mental health might limit their possibilities; others feared being marginalized or looked down on. As one millennial young man we interviewed explained, "If I had the sniffles and called in sick, no one would bat an eye. They'd *want* me to stay home. But if I admitted I needed a mental health day, I would never hear the last of it. No thanks."

While managers can't pry into their employees' mental *or* physical health in the days of HIPAA, it's always appropriate to ask if someone is okay. The goal is for team members to feel comfortable coming to their bosses with any issue relating to their well-being. A misconception, however, exists in most leaders we speak with. Since most of them can't recall the last time an employee talked to them about anxiety or depression, they assume they don't have much to worry about in that regard in their team. They also argue with us that they have pretty open lines of communication with their people, and they most likely do in most areas; yet when it comes to mental health, the lines are down. Only one in four people who suffer from anxiety say they have talked about it to their boss. The rest? They hide their symptoms. Many have been doing it since their school days.

The term "the duck syndrome" was coined at Stanford University to describe the masquerade of students at this high-pressure school, as at many colleges, working mightily to appear as though they're doing just fine, gliding calmly along like a duck on a pond, keeping up with all of their work with effortless grace. But break the surface and take a look underwater. Those graceful, smoothly gliding ducks are paddling like mad—just as these students are manically pushing themselves, frantically trying to stay afloat.

In work teams, many people who might seem to be doing fine are, in reality, in danger of going under. Just about every leader we meet is able to recount a story of a valued employee whose stress and anxiety became so problematic that they couldn't cope any longer. One leader told Chester, with clear concern, "I watched as the smartest employee I ever had slowly melted down in front of me." Ghosting has become alarmingly common. A *USA Today* poll of organizations found up to half of applicants and workers were exhibiting some type of ghosting behavior toward employers, such as blowing off interviews or not showing up for work. One manager shared with Adrian that in retrospect she had missed signs in the behavior of an employee who one day simply stopped showing up for work. He had displayed growing irritability with teammates, a drop-off in productivity, and an increase in sick days.

The signs of anxiety can sometimes be so subtle that even family and those closest to a person may be unaware. That's the case with Chris Rainey, cofounder and CEO of HR Leaders and host of a popular podcast. Rainey told us he has felt heightened levels of anxiety since childhood but hid it from everyone. "I was working in sales, in a high-pressure, *Wolf of Wall Street* type of culture. Anxiety would build up and there would be days, even weeks when I would not be able to leave my house. I'd try to walk out the door but would have an anxiety attack. I was worried: Are they going to pass me up on that promotion? Will they think I'm lying? Here's this extrovert on the phone every day who has anxiety? Right."

Rainey had been married for more than a decade, and he hadn't even been able to tell his wife. "If there was a party, I would make excuses for why I couldn't go. I felt anxious and overwhelmed in large crowds. I worried about having a panic attack, which is a vicious circle. You have anxiety about your anxiety."

Finally, just a year ago, Rainey was interviewing a guest on his podcast. Tim Munden, the chief learning officer of Unilever, was talking about mental well-being and his own PTSD. "I felt like a hypocrite," said Rainey. "Tim was very vulnerable, sharing his challenges. I decided to speak about it for the first time. It was terrifying. I knew my wife was going to hear, my employees, my cofounder, people I grew up with. But it was one of the most groundbreaking moments in my life. The weight lifted off my shoulders. It was just unbelievable."

Rainey said everyone in his life rallied to support him. Now he has the network he's needed all along. "I can say to my wife or my team that I need a break. I'm feeling overwhelmed, anxious. And they're like, sure, no problem."

This CEO today is very sensitive to those on his team who may need a break, such as mental health time off or when work needs to be taken off their plate. He's on the lookout for those who may be paddling desperately under the surface. "Sometimes it's the most confident, outgoing who are suffering on the inside. You never know," he said. "The mental energy it takes every minute of the day is exhausting. Now, I'm freed up to focus on my family, my team. I'm just so much happier at work, more productive."

Unfortunately, like Rainey did for decades, far too many employees keep quiet and may be en route to worrying themselves into early graves. That's not entirely an exaggeration. According to a study by Stanford Graduate School of Business and Harvard Business School professors, workplace stress and anxiety may be a contributing factor in more than 120,000 deaths annually. In short, tens of billions of dollars, massive employee burnout, and the mental and physical well-being of our workforces are all at stake when considering how to mitigate anxiety.

So what are organizations supposed to do about the problem? Since it's so widespread, isn't anxiety like this a result of large social forces, the effects of which companies can't hope to forestall? How is an individual manager supposed to intervene against global tensions?

Despite the objections, a growing collective of leaders we meet are finding success in helping alleviate anxiety in their teams. It's about becoming advocates for employees. To do this, they have adapted their leadership styles to be focused, first and foremost, on creating healthy places to work. Albert Einstein might have been speaking of today's best leaders when he wrote: "The measure of intelligence is the ability of change."

The Resilient

We are often invited into organizations to discuss building resilience—employees' ability to respond to change and recover from challenges. As we begin these discussions, many leaders will attribute the problem of rising anxiety levels to such things as the rapid pace of their business transformation, the intensity of competition, and a lack of toughness in people today. Few tend to consider that the ways in which they are managing their teams may not only be contributing to needless anxiety among their employees, but also sometimes the primary drivers of it.

One CEO we discussed this with admitted, "Honestly, we have used pressure as a weapon to get people to perform better. We've cranked up the anxiety more than thinking about how we could alleviate it." And yet in the same conversation, this bright leader bemoaned his company's struggle to retain capable workers and said "the ability to get and keep great talent will be the biggest differentiator in the next decade."

There's the rub. With so many employees experiencing heightened degrees of anxiety at work, leaders simply can't afford to aggravate things further, or leave team members on their own to either "buck up," "opt out," or "calm down." As a famous saying goes: "Never in the history of calming down has anyone ever calmed down by being told to calm down."

Too many managers buy into the old-school belief that it's best to let anxious workers weed themselves out: *They're just not cut out for the job* or *I don't have time to worry about everyone's mental health*, they'll confide to us. But there's simply no basis in fact that those who experience anxiety are less capable, weaker, or less valuable. In fact, it's often the opposite. Those who produce the best results are often riddled with strong feelings of anxiety. One study found 86 percent of those with high anxiety were rated as uniquely productive in their jobs. Makes sense: Employees who feel worried about not being good enough often work harder to try to prove themselves. Research also shows a large percentage of highly intelligent people experience anxiety in greater numbers than the general populace. Mensa members have been found to suffer from anxiety disorders at twice the rate of the national average.

The best leaders are beginning to understand that creating a healthy place to work can embrace those with anxiety—people who may be extremely capable and intelligent—while creating an environment that is more positive for everyone. And that can be a powerful accelerator of team success. Take the recent transformation of the England men's national football (soccer) team. Previously, England's players admitted they were so anxious about the media diatribe if they failed that it often became a self-fulfilling prophecy, as seen in 2016 when an England powerhouse team was knocked out of the European Championships by the tiny nation of Iceland. Manager Roy Hodgson stepped down at that point and a new coach was hired: quiet, unassuming former player Gareth Southgate, whose first focus would not be on tactics or fitness but on building a cohesive, positive culture. Two years later, in 2018, on the biggest stage—the World Cup—England finished in the top four, the country's best outcome in fifty-two years.

Southgate's success puts a spotlight on the new type of leaders the modern world is demanding. His style combines vulnerability with care for the individual. A student of leadership, the new manager brought in a psychologist/culture coach to work with the players. He even shared with his team his own personal experience of missing a penalty shot in Euro 96 that kept England from advancing to the championship. His willingness to discuss his setbacks and how anxiety affected him in the game has been a revolutionary concept in team management. It has liberated his players and staff to enjoy the challenge of competition rather than worry about the fear of failure and the "what if it all goes wrong" catastrophizing. Players say they now approach national team games with an excitement about showing off their skills to the world versus a fear of what might go wrong.

Mental health had never been considered as important as

technical excellence in sports, or in business for that matter, but teams are finding it is the mental game that is offering the greatest competitive advantage. Southgate was the first coach at a high level willing to talk about the anxiety that professional players face, and to help his team members by sitting down in frequent one-on-one and small-group discussions to talk through their life experiences and anxiety with compassion.

That kind of leadership is incredibly inspiring for everyone, especially for those who struggle with anxiety. And leaders need to understand how important the anxious are to the success of any organization. We find society functions because of the worrywarts in it, not despite them. Indeed, observations of our animal cousins in the wild by the famous primatologist Dian Fossey revealed that anxious chimps were pivotal to the survival of groups. They were the light sleepers, the ones who sensed danger first and sounded the alarm; they constituted a chimpanzee early warning system. In one experiment, Fossey decided to move a group's anxious chimps to another location, and when she returned a few months later she found the other apes had perished. It seems that group survival had hinged on having anxious individuals in the pack to alert the others to impending danger.

It's Beyond My Purview. Right?

It's easy to assume that some employees arrive at the workplace more able to bounce back from stressful situations than others, whether by nature or upbringing, and that there's nothing much a leader can do to build up a person's resilience. Admittedly, certain folks do seem to keep going, no matter what life throws at them, and there's fascinating science attempting to identify why some of us humans are more naturally resilient than others. For instance, although nearly everyone suffers negative events over a lifetime—job loss, divorce, hospitalization, and so on—people respond to traumas very differently. Psychologists point to two crucial factors that often separate those who are able to recover faster: mastery and social support.

Not to be confused with optimism or learning to "grin and bear it," mastery refers to the ability of individuals to see themselves as having a degree of control and influence over their lives—no matter what comes their way. The concept is so important to the U.S. Army that it offers soldiers and their families a ten-day course on resilience training, with intensive sessions designed to help those who might go into stressful situations such as combat, or those who send a loved one off to war. Participants learn to counter negative self-talk with more proactive and rational thinking patterns, be grateful for the good things that occur each day, and better concentrate on current tasks to stay in the present. Through exercises, soldiers also learn how to avoid unhealthy coping mechanisms, such as psychologically minimizing events that happen to them.

Second, respondents who report supportive social ties are more likely to recover from trauma faster and more successfully. When friends, family, or colleagues are unreceptive and critical of a person's attempt to share feelings about trauma, it increases the risk of PTSD. "Researchers believe the negative impact likely arises from attempts to discourage open communication, which increases cognitive avoidance and suppression of trauma-related memories, social withdrawal, and self-blame," says Dr. Denise Cummings, a research psychologist at the University of Illinois.

It's good for us all to remember that we cannot point to someone's life experience to explain a lack of resilience or their anxiety. Anxiety can affect anyone at any point in their life. Many people who experience anxiety didn't have particularly challenging childhoods. And for the many who do experience it, most won't feel it all the time or at the same intensity throughout their lives.

Yet as renowned University of Pennsylvania psychologist Martin Seligman's research showed, despite whatever difficulties we may have faced in the past, every one of us can develop more resilience, learn how to better bounce back from setbacks, and stay the course through tough times.

There can be enormous benefits when leaders help those who work for them overcome hurdles and setbacks. A high school principal once said to Adrian, "It may seem ironic, but the kids I worry about the most in life never get into trouble in school; they *never* get sent to my office. They grow into adults who've never had to pick up the pieces and realize that life goes on after you mess up, and that it's okay."

Of course, helping grown-ups do this can be a challenge.

Some workers become prone to coping mechanisms when things go bad—such as defensiveness and aversion to advice; withdrawal from participation; and, in extreme cases, ghosting. In fact, it's a good rule of thumb to assume that an anxious employee may jump there very quickly. Anthony offers a great bit of advice for leaders: "When you say you want to meet with someone, no matter what it's about, don't leave them wondering if they are out the door. Because many will. People aren't ignorant to unstable economic climates or the practice of silent layoffs. Specifically explaining that you want to meet tomorrow to go over revisions to a report, or whatever, is going to save your people a day of worry that could be spent productively."

In all of this, we are not suggesting leaders should try to become therapists. Can you imagine? It's vital that we turn to specialists to provide counseling; and for employees feeling anxiety symptoms at any level, referral to a company employee assistance program (EAP) or a licensed counselor can be extremely helpful. Managers can play an active role in finding the help their people need, and formal programs can have huge payoffs. PricewaterhouseCoopers has found, for example, that for every $1 invested in mental health programs, organizations receive an average return on investment of $2.30, seen through improved productivity, fewer compensation claims, reduced absenteeism, and reduced presenteeism (showing up for work even when sick, overly fatigued, or otherwise not operating at normal levels of productivity).

Forbes reports the total cost of overall poor employee health at more than $530 billion in the US alone, with much of that attributed to impaired performance. Harvard Medical School research adds that the mental health aspect of wellness has usually been overlooked in that analysis. The mindset that mental wellness is the responsibility solely of the employee and does not need to be considered by an employer is not a financially sound decision, the Harvard researchers explain. "In the long term, costs spent on mental health care may represent an investment that will pay off not only in healthier employees, but also for the company's financial health."

So, to be perfectly clear, we're big fans of offering mental health assistance. But EAP referrals and formal internal programs aren't the only answer. Managers have an important role to play as well. After all, a team is a tight social network with its own dynamic. As leaders working in an unpredictable time, we have to be particularly sensitive to the fact that our team might be more vulnerable to anxiety. Encouraging people to be open about their struggles and lending an ear as a boss can do much good. As one young worker confided to us, "Nine times out of ten when we complain we just want to be heard, and it doesn't involve advice or problem-solving. Just, 'That sounds really hard. I can't imagine going through that. I'm here for you.' We want an advocate in our boss, not someone who is *tolerant* of the issue."

Peter Diaz, CEO of the Workplace Mental Health Institute, points out that managers can "have a default to [refer everyone to an] EAP," which often leaves employees with wrong impressions. Imagine you have a best friend with anxiety, Diaz says, "and you say: 'Why don't you talk to someone else.' Or, 'Go take medication.' How long would they be your friend? People need to have a good relationship with their manager." He adds that leaders convey a counterproductive message when the only means of assistance they offer is sending their people *away* from the company. The message is: Work is toxic; you need to get the heck out of here to heal.

Why, he asks, would anyone come back to your team or company if they think it's the problem?

Diaz isn't suggesting that people suffering from heightened anxiety shouldn't speak to a therapist; he fully endorses therapy. But he argues that managers must take responsibility and do what they can to alleviate some of the strains work life is placing on so many of their people. "It's like we are blaming the individuals for having issues," he says. "What about us? Are we supporting them? Am I approachable as a manager? Am I scared of the issue?"

There's the heart of it: Are managers willing to be present with an employee as that person makes sense of their mental health issue? Do they know how far to help without it becoming a counseling session? This is vital knowledge for managers these days.

At Kraft Heinz Company, Shirley Weinstein, head of Global Rewards, says if the global pandemic of 2020 had one heartening result, it was the realization to managers at all levels that anxiety is a real business issue. "They're home with family, feeling the additional pressures and the need to stay connected with their teams. They experienced it; a realization that mental well-being is a real concern," she said.

Weinstein added, "We want our leaders to help with their employees' anxiety and emotional well-being, which is compounded with today's uncertainty. However, there's still this lingering stigma on mental health. Do I raise my hand and say, 'I need help'? When you look at EAPs, utilization is not increasing even in the midst of the pandemic. There is a concern: 'If I tell my manager, how will they react? What are they going to do?' And have we properly coached our managers on what they should do?"

To help address this very real issue, one of the leadership principles at Kraft Heinz is "Empathy and Care." Weinstein says that managers must learn to understand and diagnose what their employees are facing, "whether that be workload, work-life balance, mental health, stress, burnout, anxiety, or reduced energy levels. We are thinking about how we make sure our managers are equipped to recognize the situation, where they may be contributing to the problem, and how best to address the issues with empathy and care. We haven't completely cracked that nut yet, but we have started the conversation."

The hopeful news this book offers is that leaders of teams can adopt a set of eight simple practices we've identified that can greatly reduce the anxiety their people are feeling. Using these practices and the lessons throughout the book will help any leader convey that they genuinely care about those they are privileged to lead—sending them home each night feeling a little more valued, listened to, and included. The examples from leaders we've worked with will show the results can be profound.

As we all adjust to a world deeply affected by the coronavirus pandemic, with heightened sensitivity that even the most successful organizations with solid growth plans and seemingly secure markets may face sudden upheaval at any time, these methods for nurturing employee resilience are needed now more than ever.

Eight Strategies

We have spent twenty years coaching individual managers and their teams about how to improve the work experience and organizational culture. Our research partners have helped us survey more than one million employees over the last decade, and we've seen powerful effects can be achieved by making easily implemented adjustments in how leaders manage. To assist specifically with the pressing challenges of rising anxiety levels, we've taken a deep dive into the science of what provokes anxiety in order to identify the management practices that have the greatest capacity to relieve it.

From Adrian: My passion for this project has been fueled by my son, Anthony, who has helped write this book, investing it with rich perspective from one who has struggled intensely with the problem. Tony has suffered from severe anxiety since he was a child, but he was nonetheless able to graduate with honors from university as a biotechnology major. He excelled in tough classes like organic chemistry, physics, and bioinformatics, all while working part-time in an NIH-funded genetics lab and as a teaching assistant.

We had many conversations throughout his undergraduate years about times when he felt he had become disconnected from his job or classes, despite his passion for the subjects and the experiments being conducted. Notwithstanding many late nights of studying and a passion to work for months at a time with no weekends off, he would now and then talk about how he felt he was going nowhere. In retrospect, these conversations screamed the duck syndrome. Many of our talks became reference points that showed up all too often in the stories told to us by workers who have recounted their anxiety.

As Adrian and Chester have discussed things with Anthony, seeking deeper insight into what has enabled him to consistently achieve, we realized that in working with someone with anxiety, we could look to help build resilience in a set of specific ways. That was a lightbulb moment that set the three of us on this quest.

In the ensuing years, we've heard so much from managers about the problem, and we began to understand that we could help them solve it.

We appreciate that the prospect of plunging into what to know about anxiety as a leader is daunting, so we've done the plunging for you. The last thing any of us need is more heavy lifting. The goal with this work has been to create a simple guide for managers that they can read very quickly, providing practices to implement immediately.

We've organized the book by the eight leading sources of anxiety in the workplace, with a chapter for each strategy. They address such anxiety-inducing issues as:

+ Employees' uncertainty about the organization's strategy for contending with challenges, and how it affects job security.

+ Work overload and the need for managers to help balance loads and help prioritize.

+ A lack of clarity about prospects for career growth and development, as well as the need for clarity in everyday work situations.

+ How perfectionism has become the enemy of getting things done.

+ Fear of speaking up, contributing, and debating issues.

+ Feeling marginalized as "others" for women, people of color, those on the LGBTQ+ spectrum, and religious minorities.

+ Being excluded socially by team members, with the sense of alienation from working remotely an emerging variation of this problem.

+ A lack of confidence and feeling undervalued.

Some of us tend to be more troubled by one or two of these issues more than others, and it takes creativity on the part of a leader to help. One worker in your care may become extremely anxious about tight project deadlines. His challenge might be more about his perfectionism than feeling like there's too much work. It's the fear of *how well* he can do something that's eating at him, not how much he has to do and by when. Another employee may be entirely confident in the quality of her work but be stressed because she's seen signs of trouble ahead for the team, or organization, and is not at all confident that management has a plan to address the issues, or what her role will be given this uncertain future. As leaders, once we know what to look for, we can more effectively begin addressing the problem with the solutions provided here. And we won't just share what to do, we'll illustrate *how*, using examples of real managers and their employees.

Here's one quick story to give you a taste. Dr. Ken Huey, CEO of Red Mountain Colorado residential treatment facility, told us of a new hire in his company who missed two important appointments her first week on the job. He said, "I was thinking, 'Is this going to work out?' My business partner and I had an honest discussion with her, and she admitted she'd had panic attacks before these appointments. She had gone home and told us she had an upset stomach.

"We recruited her because she could bring important skills to our team," Huey said, "so we decided to work on ways to relieve her anxiety. When tasks felt like too much, we turned them over to others. The good news is she felt incredibly embraced by what we did, and she's not had another panic attack at work. She's also been able to accomplish all we'd hoped."

As Huey gave us this account, we noted that perhaps his worker had felt that physical symptoms would be seen as more real than mental ones (though at times anxiety can certainly manifest in physical sickness). We wondered if she had, in the past, a manager who dismissed her mental health—prompting her to avoid the true issues she was facing. The good news is that Huey was astute at listening, took the time to understand what the problem was, and found inspired ways to help.

*   *   *

Working to make team members feel understood, accepted, and secure is an extraordinary team-bonding opportunity. Research leaves not the slightest doubt that it's also a powerful productivity booster. Devoting a little extra time and attention to this new way of managing will pay off in spades, and that is a great anxiety reliever for leaders as well, many of whom are concerned with their own job security. According to management consulting firm McKinsey, "numerous studies show that in a business-as-usual environment, compassionate leaders perform better and foster more loyalty and engagement by their teams. However, compassion becomes especially critical during a crisis."

Of course, none of us is immune to the pressures and threats pervading work life these days. And employees aren't going to entirely stop feeling worry, stress, or anxiety, no matter what we do; and there is little managers can do about many of the challenges that are buffeting workplaces today. The pace of change is not going to slacken, and the competition isn't going away. But within our teams, we can go a long way to relieving tensions, providing support, inspiring enthusiasm and loyalty, and creating a safe place for people to spend their days.

Having a healthy workplace is a goal we can all feel good about.

How Anxiety  Fills the Gap

HELP TEAM MEMBERS DEAL WITH UNCERTAINTY

If you aren't suffering from anxiety, you aren't paying attention.

—Comment from an interview with a forty-seven-year-old man

Few things cause more anxiety than the unknown, and few things generate more unknowns than our modern workplaces. And the biggest unknown of all: whether our jobs will last.

By July 2020, 60 percent of American workers said they were concerned about job security. From the younger workers we interviewed, even before the pandemic, we found job fears are leading to a generation in perpetual angst. Ashley, a twenty-six-year-old who works in financial services, told us her anxiety is tied to job stability. "My generation's experience has been affected by what's happened over the past twenty years:

9/11, people got laid off; the crash of 2008, same thing. Now it's AI and robots that are making our jobs unnecessary."

In his book *Kids These Days*, journalist Malcolm Harris argues millennials are putting in more hours and producing their work more efficiently for corporations but are receiving less in return. Young people, he says, "take on the costs of training ourselves (including student debt), we take on the costs of managing ourselves as freelancers or contract workers, because that's what capital is looking for. We're not individuals, not as far as bosses are concerned. The vast majority of us are (replaceable) workers."

While that might sound harsh or a touch Marxist to some leaders, we've found Harris's views are not that extreme in his generation. Under promise of anonymity, we interviewed dozens of millennials and Gen Zers for this book—most of whom are college-educated, working professionals—and it was eye-opening. The majority expressed views that so far capitalism has let them down: They get less pay, fewer benefits, less support, and less security than prior generations. In fact, the fear of being laid off is a big reason workers agree to 24/7 availability, checking their phones at three in the morning or on vacation. They are driven by fear, and fear is indistinguishable from a threat in certain parts of our brains, especially the limbic system. When this part of the brain determines that a threat is present, an alert response is activated. Rather than helping us focus on how to improve a situation, an alert response too often leads to preoccupation with what might go wrong and indecision about what course to take, and that can lead to chronic stress.

While some leaders believe economic, job, or competitive uncertainty and resulting stress will get their people fired up for a challenge, that's simply not the case for a large portion of the workforce. Uncertainty triggers diverse physical responses in people, with often detrimental consequences on performance. Consider how it affected two professional basketball players.

Sam Cassell was a terrific free-throw shooter on any given day, averaging 86.1 percent throughout his NBA career. Yet in clutch situations, a) overtime or b) a game with less than five minutes to play and neither team ahead by more than five points, Cassell shot a remarkable 95.5 percent! When things were uncertain, Cassell had ice in his veins.

He, however, is an exception, not the rule.

Compare Cassell with another player, a six-time All-Star whose name we won't mention (he's a lot bigger than us). This player averaged about 20 points and 10 rebounds a game during the prime of his long career, and he shot free throws at about the NBA average of 75 percent. And yet in clutch situations his free-throw percentage dropped to just over 50 percent. The guy could flat-out play during regular games. But when uncertainty reigned, the chances of him sinking a free throw were no better than the flip of a coin.

The point for leaders: It's important to understand the effects of uncertainty on your people and assign the right team members to the right tasks. Those bosses who tell us their people need to "get comfortable with uncertainty" are out of touch with human psychology. Some employees may do quite well, and even thrive, in uncertain times and with assignments with a degree of ambiguity—developing a new business line with no established policies or procedures, as one example. But many people will never get comfortable or do their best work in those environments, yet they can do extremely well with tasks that have structure and known rules.

It is common today for many workers to feel intense and rising worry about a myriad of uncertain issues, from big picture challenges like pandemics and how they will affect their companies, to smaller issues such as "What is my boss really looking for in this report?" or "Am I using the right procedure for this workflow?"

The fact is, this rising generation is a much more anxious group as a whole. Some have termed them "generation paranoia." Today's young people tend to be obsessed with safety and, even before COVID-19, were troubled by a pervasive sense of threat. In the *Atlantic*, Ashley Fetters described a generation of young people who scan any room they enter for exit points and game out how they'd survive an active-shooter scenario. Can you imagine trying to work, let alone relax, in a world like that?

Leaders must also be aware of the oft-consuming worries of their people about career choices, a lack of opportunity to progress in a job, not to mention the overwhelming fears of losing one's position. One millennial summed it up for us in an interview: "The concept of not being worried about job security is entirely foreign to me." He's not alone. Four times as many millennials as Gen Xers list "fear of losing job" as one of their top concerns at work, according to *Forbes*.

Uncertainty is intensified when managers at all levels don't communicate clearly, precisely, and consistently about challenges facing their organizations—and how those issues may affect their people. We'd all have to admit that the pace of change in business has accelerated considerably, and organizations get disrupted faster than ever. For workers there is also so much information available online about how the firm is doing, and most of it is usually not positive. And yet most leaders haven't adapted their communication approach or frequency to help control the resulting anxiety overload or temper negative outside voices.

While there may be little that an individual manager can do to address the root causes of big-picture uncertainty, what they *can* do is communicate about what they know of challenges and what the organization is doing to address them, and especially how those challenges may impact their team and their priorities.

Liz Wiseman, author of *Multipliers* and a former Oracle global leader, told us, "Whether we are facing a pandemic, social injustice, or just because there's too much to know today, the job of the leader is to say to their people, 'Come with me into the dark. Together, we are going to navigate our way through complexity, uncertainty, ambiguity, and volatility to a better place.' A leader harnesses the collective intelligence of the team to find answers along the way."

The challenge most leaders have, however, is a reluctance to admit they don't have it all figured out. What Wiseman describes is a very different way of thinking about leadership.

The Power of Directness

In the midst of the pandemic of 2020, FYidoctors president Darcy Verhun committed to what he called "constant communication transparency."

FYidoctors operates more than 250 optometry clinics in Canada from coast to coast and was just entering the United States when, due to COVID-19, the company was forced to temporarily close all its clinics—except to provide emergency eye care—in order to follow public health guidelines. "To keep everyone informed during this stressful period we held daily updates, via Zoom, with our entire team, which is close to three thousand colleagues," Verhun told us. "Ahead of the calls the executive team would spend time thinking through our team members' uncertainty and what they might be feeling. We led these calls from our home office boardroom. We wanted to signal to our emergency care givers that we were prepared to do what we were asking them to do by being in the office throughout the pandemic while following medical authority guidelines.

"At the start of every call we would reconfirm our plan, what key issues we were working on for that day along with what had changed since the previous day's call. Every day was fluid and dynamic. What we were living through was incredibly stressful for everyone and, as the calls unfolded, questions would pour in via chat to the executive team. We would at times interrupt each other and tackle a question on the fly. We had to think fast to respond openly and transparently. In being willing to do this we built trust, confidence, and deep engagement with the team."

Said Verhun, a few weeks in, the executives found that they no longer were the only ones responding to queries. "Our doctors and team began to mentor each other and answer each other's questions faster than we could read them in the chat. That told us that everybody was helping build solutions and helping to lead collectively to the goals the leadership team had identified for the organization. This was only possible because of the clarity provided up front and the unwavering guiding principles and values our entire team understood that we used to make decisions."

By midyear, FYidoctors clinics were opening back up and the company was reporting its best monthly results and growth in its twelve-year history.

One need look no further than the decline of Yahoo for an example of how detrimental a lack of transparency can be to morale during uncertain times. Despite an optimistic outward appearance to investors, employees had begun doubting the company's viability by the mid-2010s. According to *New York Times* interviews with Yahoo employees, leaders had embarked on a series of "stealth layoffs." They called in a handful of people each week and fired them quietly. No one knew who would be safe or who would be gone next, and fear paralyzed many workers. The entire process was confusing and demoralizing to loyal employees who loved the company and believed in its platforms. "We all want to make as much impact as we can and leverage Yahoo's existing strengths," employee Austin Shoemaker said at the time, summing up the feelings of many loyal Yahoos.

Finally, in March 2015, CEO Marissa Mayer told the staff at an all-hands event that the bloodletting was over. She even darkly joked that no one would be laid off that week. Yet shortly thereafter, more cuts began.

Employees were well aware of how fierce Yahoo's competition was. The company was also struggling with an industry-wide drop in display advertising, not to mention a challenge in trying to excel at so many things—from news and sports to web searches and email. But employees interviewed said they wanted to face the hurdles as a cohesive team, even if that meant that some might have to depart the company for it to survive. While Mayer tried to hide layoffs behind the euphemism "remixes," one employee told the *New York Post*: "I don't think people want to be mollified. They want to be respected and trusted with facts so they can plan their lives, and also help."

In just about any company, long before news reports emerge of product failures, layoffs, mergers, or downturns, most employees clue in that the firm is facing challenges. In uncertain times, anxiety (and often apathy) is amped up when managers don't talk transparently about issues and what the company is doing about them.

Take General Electric as another unfortunate case during the tenure of CEO Jeffrey Immelt. Employees began to understand the company was facing serious issues long before the public was aware of them. And yet a "success theater" masked challenges for years at the multinational. Sources on the inside told the *Wall Street Journal* their topmost leader didn't want to hear any bad news, and executives continued to project an optimism that didn't always match the reality of their operations or market. In May 2017, in front of a room of Wall Street analysts, Immelt said, "This is a strong, very strong company," and then defended GE's profit goals. "It's not crap. It's pretty good really. . . . Today, when I think about where the stock is compared to what the company is, it's a mismatch."

It *was*. But not in the direction he was talking about. While GE shares were trading near $28 that day, less than two years later they would drop below $6.

We have watched as new CEO Larry Culp has instilled a revitalized culture at GE where internal and external stakeholders clearly understand the strategy, and where employees can raise tough issues and know they will be addressed honestly and directly. Six months into the job, we were heartened to hear Culp explain, "What we're going to try to do is to share with people, in as transparent a way as we possibly can, what the issues are and the plan that we have. But it will take time. And we don't want to sugarcoat this."

Like Culp, other leaders around the world are trying to involve employees as partners in this process of working through uncertainty. For instance, by 2013, executives at AT&T had concluded that 100,000 of their 280,000 workers were in jobs that would most likely not be relevant in as little as a decade. Like many companies in the technology sector, AT&T faced a future in which its legacy businesses were quickly becoming obsolete. With an industry moving from cables and hardware to the internet, cloud, and data science, AT&T leaders knew the company had to reinvent itself. They communicated the pending challenges with employees and displayed a commitment to try to retrain workers, not wanting to abandon the knowledge and passion their people had.

Since 2013, AT&T has spent some $250 million each year on employee education and professional development programs, not to mention more than $30 million annually on tuition assistance. By 2018 the company estimated that half of its employees were actively engaged in acquiring skills for newly created roles. People who'd been retrained were filling half of all technology management jobs and received half of all promotions.

Network support specialist Jacobie Davis has been with AT&T for more than twenty years in a variety of positions from sales to 911-line maintenance. Given the transition to a software focus at the company, he repositioned his skills to earn a spot as a product development engineer in cloud-based test environments. He said, "It's really hard to describe the vast difference between the things we're moving toward and the types of legacy technology I've been working on. It's like night and day." (We introduce a Skill Development Model to help with this process in Chapter 4.)

Here's a company that understood that huge layoffs would undermine trust in management, trust that was necessary for employee engagement, innovation, and performance. Since the inception of this talent overhaul, and in large part by communicating truthfully with and retraining its workforce, from 2013 through 2019 AT&T increased revenue from $129 billion to $181 billion, reduced its product-development cycle time while accelerating time-to-revenue, and even made *Fortune*'s 100 Best Companies to Work For list for the first time.

If executives at a company aren't employing an honest and clear approach like this, team leaders may have limits about what they can share to help reduce uncertainty, but within those limits we find there's much they can do. In an interview we conducted with Columbia Business School professor Rita McGrath, she said this involves managers trying to absorb as much uncertainty as possible, instead of pushing it onto their people (admittedly this might increase managers' own anxiety levels somewhat, but leaders typically can accept a lot more risk than their people).

McGrath cited an example of a product development team at an insurance company she was working with. As background, insurance in America is regulated state by state, so whether a new product can be launched in a particular state depends on the state regulatory committee. The project lead,

Bill, asked his contact in operations, Todd, if his team would be ready to launch the new product they had been developing, but Todd hemmed and hawed. Dr. McGrath had to explain to Bill that he would need to be specific and let operations know how many US states they needed to be ready to launch in. "But we don't know yet," Bill said. McGrath said that in his leadership role, Bill could more afford to be wrong than his lower-level operations contact. The project leader went back to Todd and said, "I expect you to be ready for fifteen states." The conversation immediately changed for the better. Todd said his team could handle that, and even twenty states if they borrowed resources.

While some degree of unknown about one's work is inevitable, what this example illustrates is that managers may be able to fill gaps for their team members with clarity, even in volatile circumstances.

In this chapter, we will introduce a series of six methods managers can use to help team members deal with uncertainty about big-picture issues, such as potential threats to the organization. First, however, we will discuss the most important issue leaders should communicate about to reduce uncertainty: individual performance and development.

Communicating Frequently One-on-One

A good deal of employee anxiety is about their own performance and growth opportunities. In other words: *How am I doing?* and *Do I have a future here?* Managers create more ambiguity when they aren't clear about such things. One executive we once reported to was wont to say to us as we handed him assignments, "This just isn't it yet, but I'll know it when I see it." And then send us on our way. He thought he was giving his team "creative freedom" that would encourage our best work, but in reality he was ratcheting up anxiety to excruciating levels.

Of course, we understand there are formal methods of giving employees feedback, e.g. the annual review, but research has shown infrequent check-ins like this are woefully inadequate at addressing the uncertainty that many feel about their jobs in the six or twelve months between these meetings. Many firms have decided to either alter performance reviews or abandon them entirely, replacing them with other processes for evaluating and developing employees that are more timely, frequent, and facilitated by the immediate supervisor. We call this process the *continuous review*, a way of supplying ongoing feedback and gauging employee performance with real-time metrics.

Greg Piper, worldwide director of continuous improvement for Becton, Dickinson & Co., holds one-on-one performance and development sessions every other week for thirty minutes with each of his team members, who are all remote and spread around the globe. "'What do *you* want to talk about?' is always the first question I ask," said Piper.

Stephan Vincent, senior director of LifeGuides, a peer-to-peer support network, says he begins each day with the same question. "Every morning my first message to everyone on my

team is, how are you feeling *today?* Because today is probably different than yesterday." These check-ins before diving
in should not be rushed, and people should have time to tell
their stories if they want to share. It's up to a leader to dig
below the "fine."

"The workplace of tomorrow will be much more human,
and less transactional than it's been," Vincent added. "As
we create deeper bonds, it's ultimately going to benefit the
company with more productivity, more collaboration, more
innovation."

With all of this, note that it's never appropriate to ask
someone, "Do you have anxiety?" As Anthony explained,
"That is a privacy violation and can make things worse. Instead, consider privately asking something such as, 'I notice
you are having a hard time in these specific stressful situations. Is there anything I can do to help?'"

Evidence on the value of frequent check-ins comes from
BetterWorks research, which found employees who meet and
discuss progress toward goals with their managers *weekly* are
up to twenty-four times more likely to achieve their targets.
By providing constant reviews, managers are also able to give
tough feedback when necessary and quell anxious feelings in
many employees who are doing good work but are actually
concerned about their performance. According to a Leadership IQ survey of thirty thousand people, only 29 percent of
working adults know whether their "performance is where it
should be." Just as troubling, more than half say they *rarely*
know if they are doing a good job.

Tyler, a customer service employee we met, said he began to feel adrift after moving from a highly communicative manager to a new boss who was more tight-lipped. Not knowing what this new guy thought about his performance, or if he felt he could progress any further, Tyler finally pushed the boss for some feedback to lessen the uncertainty he was feeling. They sat down and the manager delivered some positives he had seen to date and also gave some things to work on. Tyler told us he found the improvement ideas "jarring," and ended up obsessing over the negatives. He's not alone. The human brain has a negative bias. There is a greater surge in electrical activity in our brains in response to down news than upbeat news. And it's like Velcro when we hear bad things about ourselves—even if the good outweigh the bad by ten to one. Ironically, that may have been why this manager was so loath to give feedback to any of his people in the first place.

Tyler allowed us to coach him to try something new when the pair met again. We told him to first pay attention to any and all positives the boss was saying and write them down. We told him not to focus on any weaknesses until he had captured all the manager's thinking on his good attributes. He reported back that it felt remarkably weird taking notes on the good stuff his boss was saying, and even odder to ask for clarifications on those positives; but after just ten minutes of this he began to realize that his manager was well aware of his strengths. Tyler then saw the improvement ideas his boss was offering in a new light. They were to help him develop his talents so he could progress, not an indictment of his abilities overall. He left the meeting with newfound confidence.

The lesson learned from this, that we have since passed along to the leaders we work with, is to take much more time than in the past to be very clear on your appreciation of your employees' strengths.

A complaint we hear about this is that it would take too much work on the part of managers to overcome uncertainty in each of their people—too much coaching, communicating, and hand-holding. Adrian heard this in Stockholm in late 2019 while conducting a workshop for the Nordic Forum for Continuous Improvement on how to lead cultural change. The several hundred people in attendance were from various companies all over Sweden. At one point, Adrian gave them a task intended to help brainstorm better ways to talk with their teams about change and improve information flow up and down in complex environments. In the debrief, one older manager complained about the younger generation: "Leading them is hard because they want *excessive* amounts of direction and feedback."

Sitting at the very next table were a pair of fresh-faced younger workers, clearly still in their twenties. So Adrian asked them, "Do *you* need excessive amounts of direction and feedback?"

The group chuckled, and one of the two young people spoke up with characteristic Swedish tact. "I don't think that's entirely accurate," she said. "I believe what I need is *consistent* direction and feedback." Ah, the wisdom of youth!

Usually when employees fail to adapt to change or refuse to push boundaries, we find that they are afraid of the consequences to their jobs, even though they may be more than capable of going beyond what is asked, modifying their behavior, or pushing the status quo. Since leaders don't clearly ask for more out of them, these people never do any more than asked. Worse, they don't speak up when they should.

In an interview we conducted for this book with Dr. Amy Edmondson of Harvard Business School and author of *The Fearless Organization*, she explained, "When people feel heightened interpersonal anxiety, they worry, 'Will I get in trouble if . . . ?' or 'Will I get rejected if . . . ?' Psychological safety represents an absence of interpersonal anxiety—the 'What do you think of me?' anxiety, which is so prevalent in the human experience and can get in the way of people doing the right thing, from offering up an idea to averting a crisis by speaking up."

Clarity from managers in one-on-one settings gives workers a sense of what's allowable and what's not, and what kind of actions are necessary in the moment. It also helps employees take on new projects or oversee tasks, because they understand the parameters of their new responsibilities and what freedoms in decision-making they do and don't have.

Here's an illustration. We once visited with Brett Fischer, who was director of merchandising for Major League Soccer's Real Salt Lake, the day after his team had hosted a playoff match. Fischer had assigned a friendly, outgoing worker named Lisa to tend one of the cash registers in the team store.

Fischer had been busy, and in giving Lisa the assignment he simply said, "Work your magic," and off he ran to other matters.

Lisa began chatting with each customer in line, asking them a question, telling a funny story here and there. On this huge game day, her friendly conversations were slowing the line to a crawl. Fischer pulled Lisa aside and said, "I wasn't clear. This is on me. Normally it's great that you talk with customers. But today, we need a sense of urgency at the register. Here are our options: We can put someone else up front and allow you to engage with customers on the floor, or you need to focus on getting that till to go a hundred miles an hour."

At first, he said, Lisa was defensive and hurt. "She thought I was criticizing her as a person," he said. Her anxiety was ratcheted up. But Fischer clarified to Lisa that speed was what their clients needed on this very busy day. She eventually said, "I want to stay on the register."

Fischer checked on Lisa several times in the hours that followed, and her line was humming. "By the end of the game, she left feeling like a million bucks," he said.

This was, admittedly, a modest interaction. But aren't most in a team? Fischer had created ambiguity and was big enough to admit his mistake. He attempted to diffuse a potentially anxiety-charged situation by providing a business focus, gave honest but kind feedback, and helped Lisa see what customers needed instead of making her feel she had failed.

He learned that by giving clear guidance about what's expected up front, employees can start the race in a much more effective gear.

Despite the advantages of clear, regular one-on-one communication, many managers still express frustration that their people want that kind of guidance. Instead, they hope their team members will act with more autonomy. It's true that a degree of autonomy is not only vital for efficacy but for feelings of empowerment, and no one enjoys being micromanaged. But managers typically have a lot of know-how and valuable examples to share about ways they've tackled the work their people are doing. When they don't take the time to share that wisdom, they can raise anxiety levels considerably.

With the very specific ways in which firms operate today, and unique platforms for almost every team, getting things right is truly in the details. Providing the minutiae may seem tedious, but leaders should consider how they'd approach tasks as if it were for the first time. Many of the mundane details they might rush through may become the focal point of important conversations with their team members.

Six Methods to Meet Uncertainty Head-On

From our work coaching leaders, we have developed a set of methods that any manager can use to communicate with employees to help reduce uncertainty. These methods include ways to help team members feel needed and engaged by meeting regularly with them as a group to discuss and debate industry changes and how those might affect their team; incorporating active ways of listening to concerns and suggestions from employees one-on-one; and developing metrics to measure success at helping people feel informed about potential challenges the organization is facing and involved in seeking solutions.

Method 1: Make It Okay to Not Have All the Answers

When Lutz Ziob was general manager of Microsoft Learning, he led his team of four hundred employees through a significant transformation. For years, his externally focused learning organization had made their money inside client corporations, teaching workers how to use the Microsoft toolkit. The company had a multibillion-dollar operation based around this business model. With an eye to the horizon, the debate became whether to let go of this profitable way of doing things and instead start training people in Microsoft products much earlier, in university or high school. Ziob didn't have the answers, so he turned to his people and introduced a structured way to debate.

He asked team members to come to a series of discussions with evidence and a point of view. They were to defend their opinion vehemently, and then be willing to switch sides. Chris, for instance, would argue against the change from a sales perspective, and Lee Anne in the affirmative from a marketing perspective. Then Ziob would have the two switch sides and continue the discussion. Explained bestselling author Liz Wiseman, "In the end it was hard to know who won debates. It didn't matter. The switch obfuscated the 'who' part of it."

Ziob mitigated as much uncertainty as he could, and built

a team that thrived by providing the best information available and an environment for his team to analyze their future and make informed decisions as a group. In interviewing his direct reports, Wiseman told us, "to a person they said that their leader created a learning environment where people could experiment, take risks, and make mistakes. It is what allowed their team to make intelligent decisions in times of uncertainty."

Method 2: Loosen Your Grip in Tough Times

In an interview with Nicole Malachowski, the first female pilot in the U.S. Air Force demonstration squadron the Thunderbirds, she explained how pilots fly when turbulence or headwinds occur. "It's human nature to try to resist change. When we are flying in formation three feet apart, at 450 miles per hour, upside down, we have a contract with each other. It's to loosen your grip. If you fly with your hand on the stick with all five fingers tight, and you try to react to every bump, you get into what we call a pilot-induced oscillation. Bigger corrections. It's unsafe and makes things worse. That's not how you nurture change. When things get bumpy, we lighten up on the stick, using just a few fingers."

Unfortunately, research shows more than half of workers say their managers become more closed-minded and controlling during ambiguous, high-pressure situations. Malachowski's analogy is a terrific way to think about leading a team through uncertainty. If we, as leaders, fight change or try to control every aspect of our employees' work during a crisis, we'll typically make things worse. If leaders stay loose—open and curious—they'll be more successful in the long run and keep their teams together.

Reimagine the scenario with Brett Fischer and Lisa. It was certainly a very busy day in the store and the pressure was on Brett, as the manager, to deliver. Instead of taking a few minutes to have that caring, focused one-on-one with Lisa, picture what would have happened if he had tried to micromanage her—perhaps motioning from across the room to speed things up with a few twists of his hand, or by taking over himself, or by giving her overcomplicated instructions about how to behave from then on.

How often do we, as leaders, start to micromanage when things get tense?

Tasha Eurich, an organizational psychologist who writes on self-awareness and suffers from anxiety herself, told us that leaders must live in the moment during a crisis. "There's such uncertainty. During the pandemic, for instance, we worry, when will there be a vaccine, when will I get to go back to the office? We don't know. What I can control is the day that I have, or the moment that I have, and that lessens my experience of stress.

"If you have anxiety, every evening before you go to bed your mind is racing, so I force myself to think about what tomorrow could look like at its best. Realistic expectations: Perhaps I'll get a call from an old friend or an inquiry to work with a client. You are engineering hope and optimism. You are saying to yourself, 'Everything is going to be okay.'"

Following up on Dr. Eurich's comment, note that it's more than appropriate for team leaders to, now and then, let their teams know that they are overwhelmed and might need a little help. This kind of vulnerability as the boss—admitting anxiety—will go a long way to helping your people open up when they need help themselves.

Method 3: Ensure Everyone Knows Exactly What's Expected of Them

This may sound basic, but when employees don't understand what is needed of them day-by-day, it's like throwing fuel on the anxiety fire. Managers may respond to this suggestion by saying, "Of course my people know what they're supposed to get done! They've got job descriptions, deliverables. They've got KPIs and targets to meet." Each person should have a set of specific goals. Yet time and again, team members we visit with say they suffer from a lack of clarity about what's really expected of them or how they are doing regarding their goals.

From the workers we interviewed for this book, we can attest that much anxiety stems from details about their jobs that managers often assume to be insignificant. A rule: If an employee is asking questions about minutia, they're unfamiliar with a process. Indeed, several of our young interviewees complained about the on-the-job trainings they'd received, which were more overviews and not tailored to how someone in their position would use the software or follow a procedure or implement a system. Said our millennial Anthony: "With some jobs I've had, I got thrown in the deep end and no one explained the details. There were a lot of times I'd think, 'Oh no, I have to ask about this for the third time. Maybe I'm just not cut out for this.' Eventually the details became second nature, which was maybe why they were never mentioned to me; but they were the hardest things for me to get."

Yes, people may have goals, but, as Anthony described: Anxiety can be ratcheted up when employees are not given enough guidance about *how* to achieve their goals; when no one takes the time to show them approaches that have been most effective or warn them of common mistakes to avoid; or when a manager does not help them deal with challenges that emerge.

Another young employee confided to us, "I would kill to have my boss take a few minutes now and then to help prioritize all that's going on and maybe give me an idea of how much latitude I have to make my own decisions." That comment bears rereading for all of us in leadership.

In many cases, bosses think they *are* clearly communicating their expectations, when in reality, they aren't being clear at all. This can cause workers to stall or misfire. But the best leaders, when they realize they aren't being clear, accept responsibility, allow themselves to be corrected, then do what they can to more clearly explain what is needed.

And when times are uncertain, targets should be shortened considerably, says Deepak Nachnani, CEO and founder of human capital management company peopleHum. "Thinking too far in the future causes stress, which raises anxiety levels. When we are in survival mode in our company, we set weekly goals. 'What are we going to do next week?' You don't talk about long-term goals then; you keep people working on very short-term targets so they don't have a chance to have negative thoughts come into their minds."

Method 4: Keep People Focused on What Can Be Controlled

Some of the factors that will affect an employee's performance, and the future of any team or business, are simply beyond any individual's control. An economic downturn will most likely impact sales; a failure of a key supplier will slow your production and deliveries to clients. When team members concentrate their thoughts on what they can't control, anxiety grows. Part of effective leadership is about helping workers acknowledge what they cannot change and direct their attention to what they *can* change. That's a better tension reliever than a session of acupuncture.

We visited once with a customer service team. The department was assigned part of the US as a territory. During a focus group session, employees identified the company's antiquated system for managing workflow as a pain point. None of the team members could keep up with demand. They were incredibly frustrated.

Despite that, however, the team achieved high marks for the *quality* of their work. The employees told us how appreciative they were of their team leader, who was effective in relieving anxiety about keeping up on the expectations for speed.

She coached her workers to accept that the system was what it was, and other regions of the country weren't any faster. She encouraged her people to redirect their attention to *accuracy*. She absorbed any flack from above, and helped her team focus on what they *could* get done each day. She helped them establish workable timelines and motivated them to deliver; and at the end of each week they celebrated *quality* successes.

She said, "What we can control is our work ethic, the quality of the product we deliver, and how we treat each other and our clients." What this boss had her people practice is called "emotional acceptance." She didn't try to quash feelings of stress with positive thinking, which often just makes things worse. Instead, she restructured their to-do lists to give emphasis to what they could realistically master.

Unfortunately, vague or unrealistic goals aren't uncommon nowadays. Unreachable or ambiguous targets are often used to push teams to their limits. But when no one ever reaches the mark, it can lead to burnout, disengagement, and intense anxiety about missing expectations. This leader was able to explain how each person was making valued contributions, and it made all the difference.

One way to do this is to redistribute employee to-do lists to ensure that each item contains an action verb, e.g., "*Return* phone calls within one hour." If you can't find a concrete action verb for a goal, it's a sign that the action is beyond a person's control and is likely to cause undue stress. As one example, a goal of "good phone habits are essential" is vague and will most likely cause more stress for team members.

Method 5: Have a Bias to Action

"To help our people self-regulate their anxiety, we show them how to accept risk and have a bias to action," explained Stan Sewitch, vice president of Global Organization Development for the WD-40 Company. "One of the best stress relievers—proven to be useful in reducing the sympathetic nervous system enervation—is movement. That can include intellectual movement as well as physical."

With a team-wide bias to action, employees become less afraid to make decisions and move forward, even in the face of uncertainty. In these cultures, people don't spend days, weeks, or months debating if their approach is the only logical one; they do things and realize not everything will be perfect. They are also not afraid of being held accountable for making a poor decision. This is such an important concept that "Bias for Action" is one of retail giant Amazon's core values. As that company proclaims: "Speed matters in business. Many decisions and actions are reversible and do not need extensive study. We value calculated risk taking."

Yet during uncertainty, too many people freeze and can't decide on a course to take, worried they'll be held accountable for a wrong call. Sewitch adds that leadership's role is to first tell the truth so their people have all the available information (here's what we know and what we don't), and then to encourage and guide their tribe members to move. Leaders also set the example since people believe the behaviors they observe, not the words they hear, from their leaders. "It's important to let people know where you are seeing improvement because they may not recognize it themselves. Then celebrate those wins. Finally, don't punish people for making intelligent errors, or what we call learning moments."

Explaining this concept of the "learning moment," WD-40 Company CEO Garry Ridge told us, "A learning moment is the positive or negative outcome of any decision, action, or event that is freely shared with all in order to advance the collective knowledge of our tribe." He added, "It can be a period of frustration, a burst of inspiration, a breakthrough of collaboration in which people stumble upon a problem, unearth an opportunity, or fail at an initiative, and then communicate what they've learned without fear of reprisal.

"We don't expect perfection. Pursuit of perfection does not produce great results. It just stops people from taking action or risks. We expect people to be curious, to experiment, and to get comfortable with uncertainty of outcomes."

Ridge went on to explain his own epiphany about learning moments: "When I get introduced at events, our company's reputation often precedes me. The emcee might say nice things about me, and then I say, 'Let me tell you the truth. I'm the chairman and CEO of WD-40 Company. I'm consciously incompetent about a lot of things. I'm probably wrong and roughly right at most things.'" It's clear that humility is a prerequisite in creating an organization that is not afraid to act, to learn, and to evolve.

Method 6: Offer Constructive Feedback

This is an adage that everyone commits to but few leaders practice. Offering constructive feedback builds on the process of one-on-one performance and development conversations but is so important that it merits its own method in reducing anxiety. The most effective leaders we've met are not afraid to deliver fair, tough coaching. And yet according to *Forbes*, nine out of ten managers say they avoid giving constructive feedback to their employees for fear of them reacting badly. Funny that research also shows some 65 percent of today's workers feel shortchanged when it comes to receiving individualized feedback from their bosses.

To offer constructive feedback, we steer leaders away from the commonly recommended "sandwich" approach of offering a negative between two positives. In these cases, the constructive suggestions can get suffocated under a pillow full of praise, or employees may focus only on the negatives. No, the best constructive feedback includes specific ideas for improvement, instead of generalities, along with meaningful praise in the right measure.

One of our coaching clients admitted he had never been good at giving feedback but was game to try again. One of his first attempts was with an employee who had been missing some deadlines. He recounted to us a private conversation with her. He said, "I've noticed some changes in the way you are working and your results over the past few weeks. I know how focused and driven you normally are, so I wanted to see if there was anything at all you are having trouble with that I could help with." That was terrific, we told him. He got to the point and acknowledged the issue openly without hedging, but he also let her know how valued her work was to the team. He also offered to work together with her to fix the problem.

The employee admitted to some personal struggles outside the job, and the manager was able to empathize. After listening, he offered her a couple of afternoons off to address the challenges, and together they worked on prioritizing her assignments for the coming weeks. They kept meeting weekly, and soon after she delivered a project ahead of time. We encouraged him to publicly reward that achievement, and he did in his next staff meeting. He said how proud she'd been to share with the team how she'd pulled off the win.

When we ask leaders why they aren't living up to their employees' expectations in giving clear feedback, they often tell us that it is not only uncomfortable but time-consuming. "No one wants to hear what they are doing wrong," they say. We understand. We had an employee in our corporate days who we tried to coach to collaborate better with his peers, but the fellow didn't believe he had a problem. He was a friend of the CEO, so we had to tread lightly. In our next coaching session, we gave him specifics about the kind of behaviors we were expecting, and we offered facts about when he hadn't lived up to expectations with actual things said about him by peers around the company (with their permission).

The employee was still skeptical. Why hadn't these colleagues told him themselves? He left the meeting and over the next few hours confronted each person we'd quoted. Each recanted like a prisoner on the Spanish Inquisition rack. They agreed that, yes, he was a terrific collaborator, and, yes, we must have misinterpreted what they'd said. Our employee gladly returned to his delusions.

We recognize that there is a small percentage of the human population who will never accept coaching. They want validation, not growth. Leaders can continue to patiently try to enroll these folks in the coaching process, but at some point we have to decide if they are the right fit for their roles. In this case, our uncollaborative worker was eventually "remixed" after team member complaints grew too loud to ignore (by then we had a new CEO).

Yet despite the uncoachable out there, we must persist in helping our people excel and thrive. Feedback—both positive and constructive—is necessary to developing mental toughness and resilience in team members. Constructive feedback is vital because it clarifies expectations, builds confidence that people can improve, and helps team members learn from and recover from mistakes (which we all make). It's also worth noting that with time, these conversations become less uncomfortable. When it's the norm in a team, people don't take correction as personally. It's just a part of the way the group runs, which is why these one-on-ones should be positive and genuinely constructive, not intense or awkward.

Putting the Methods Together

Doria Camaraza is senior vice president and general manager of the American Express Service Centers in Fort Lauderdale, Florida; Mexico City, Mexico; and Buenos Aires, Argentina. She has led a very large team of thousands of call center professionals through more than a decade of perpetual change and uncertainty. One of the best leaders we have worked with, Camaraza attempts to be transparent about situations facing the volatile credit card industry and commits to her people that she'll inform them as soon as she knows something may be changing. A few of the formal values she encourages her leadership team to live by include: "We communicate openly, honestly, and candidly"; "We seek solutions and not blame"; and "We try to involve people in decisions that affect them."

Camaraza shares tough news, but also gives an ample amount of hope. She explains to her employees why the company maintains a proprietary operation rather than outsourcing to a third-party call center. She lets them know what they need to maintain in terms of timeliness, accuracy, and cost.

Leaders often shy away from discussing hard truths. They fear that such a discussion might dishearten their workers or cause them to bolt. And yet, there's something exhilarating for employees about facing facts head-on. Such inclusion helps people feel like they are being brought into the inner circle to brainstorm solutions to challenges. Ambiguity either prolongs inevitable bad news or widens the trust gap. Or both.

We were particularly affected by a conversation we had with Ryan Westwood, CEO of business management firm Simplus, who spoke about the link between anxiety and uncertainty. "There is an inherent distrust in leaders today," he said. That is a powerful understanding, and we wish every manager knew how true it is. Westwood continued, "You have to prove that you can be trusted. When this pandemic hit, the first thing we did was cut the pay of the executive leadership, including myself. We communicated that early and it sent a message that we were willing to make sacrifices."

Still, three months into the crisis, the CEO and his team realized that they would have to make a few tough cuts. "We held an all-hands meeting with more than five hundred employees around the world, and I told everyone we'd tried to make it through without any layoffs, but we were going to have to, and it would affect about 3 percent of our people." He explained why the cuts were absolutely necessary—showing the numbers—and Westwood outlined the plan for those who would be affected. "It was amazing how many messages I got later that said, 'I never feel like I'm going to be blindsided here,' or 'I always feel like you're going to be honest with me.'" The actual reduction in force was only 1 percent by the end because his team rallied and was able to minimize the impact.

Openness, especially about delicate matters, is much too rare. As we consult with organizations, we find that many leaders come up short at helping employees honestly understand whether or not they have a solid future within the organization, or at what level their opportunities may top out. At one manufacturing plant, for example, the HR manager had worked for twenty years to receive the proper accreditations and certificates so that he might take over when the vice president of HR retired. When the day finally came and he sent in his application for the big job, he received a one-line email response from the CEO. It read, "We could not support you in this role." There was no warning. No face-to-face candor. Just twenty years of work and then those eight words that would shape his, his coworkers', and his family's perception of the company forever. In contrast, in interviews we conducted at the American Express call centers, we were struck by how each member of Camaraza's leadership team seemed compelled to be respectfully honest with employees about their development opportunities and career potential, even if they decided to leave because of that clarity. Asking someone to sail blindly into the future is never a good idea—for a team member or the organization.

To achieve the kind of transparency we have witnessed in the best teams, workers have to have avenues that allow them to communicate upward—not only with their team leader but with senior leadership—and know they are being heard. We've all seen fly-by attempts at connection from bosses. "Hihowareyouohgood" isn't giving anyone a warm fuzzy feeling. Without real listening, employees who might want to offer up solutions about issues the company is facing will be discouraged to even try.

A leader who was effective at this kind of upward communication was James Rogers, then president and CEO of Duke Energy. Rogers had a reputation for tackling hard topics, and he instituted "listening sessions" with groups of up to one hundred managers in three-hour meetings. You may have seen these kinds of gatherings with mixed results. Rogers's sessions worked, perhaps because he began by asking everyone to grade him anonymously on electronic voting devices on a scale of A to F. The results immediately appeared on a screen for all to see. The grades were generally good, but less than half of employees were willing to give him an A.

He took the feedback to heart and conducted this opening exercise each time they met. He would then ask open-ended questions about what they were seeing in the trenches and what he could do to help. Somewhat ironically, he found that "internal communication" was the area in which most of his managers thought he could improve upon. As Rogers found, upward feedback involves absorbing criticism even when it is direct and personal—and when those delivering it work for you. As he showed, that usually means applying the suggestions to improve your leadership style. And the only response that's appropriate or necessary at the time is "Thanks for the feedback."

Ryan Westwood holds such open feedback sessions and says they can be eye-opening. "We once created a program to give out cash incentives to employees based on them getting further certifications. Our leadership team was really excited about it, and I shared the plan with a group of employees.

They said, 'Ryan, this is crap. None of us will respond to this.' I was shocked."

Westwood asked the group what they would do instead, and with the advice he went back and the team redesigned the program. He said, "Those employees became champions because it was now *their* program. It was a huge success and we saw quadruple the number of employees getting certifications."

If there's one positive aspect of uncertainty, it's that it provides a logical rationale for why every voice is needed. Amy Edmondson of Harvard Business School told us, "If we had a perfect blueprint or a crystal ball as leaders, we wouldn't *need* to hear from our people. It's the existence of uncertainty that gives people permission to speak up, despite doubt. Uncertainty all but requires input from everyone. So as long as you acknowledge the uncertainty that lies ahead, it can be your friend in creating psychological safety."

Communication is key in the process, Camaraza said to us. "In our team we listen and we explain. There are times we can incorporate employee suggestions into our strategy and there are times we can't. There are decisions made above us that we like, and some we might not agree with as a leadership team, but you have to always explain the reasoning and listen with real intent to the feedback."

In this way, no matter what's going on—good or bad—we face uncertainty together, as a team.

Lead through Uncertainty

- Uncertainty can trigger various responses in people, often with negative consequences on performance. The most common uncertainty for today's employees is whether or not a job will last.

- Uncertainty is exacerbated when managers don't communicate enough about challenges facing their organizations and how those issues may affect their people and their teams.

- A good deal of employee uncertainty is about their own performance and development, i.e., *How am I doing?* and *Do I have a future here?* By meeting one-on-one regularly to evaluate performance and growth opportunities, leaders can help team members avoid misreading situations while enhancing their engagement and commitment to the organization.

- Leaders can use a set of methods to help reduce uncertainty: 1) make it okay to not have all the answers, 2) loosen your grip in tough times, 3) ensure everyone knows exactly what's expected of them, 4) keep people focused on what can be controlled, 5) have a bias to action, and 6) offer constructive feedback.

SUMMARY

How to Turn **3** Less into More

———

You can't calm the storm, so stop trying. What you can do is calm yourself. The storm will pass.

—Timber Hawkeye

In order to become a Navy SEAL—part of the world's most elite special forces unit—one must first pass through what is called "Hell Week." During this fourth week of basic conditioning, recruits train for five days and five nights solid, with a total of four hours of sleep.

Brandon Webb passed the challenge. While many people assume physical toughness is the secret to becoming one of the 10 to 15 percent who will graduate, he says, "What SEAL training really tests is your mental mettle. It is designed to push you mentally to the brink, over and over again, until you are hardened and able to take on any task with confidence, regardless of the odds—or until you break."

According to Columbia Business School professor Rita McGrath, author of *Seeing Around Corners*, researchers have found two archetypes of behavior in those who attempt to pass SEAL training. First are called the "Taskers," who look to complete each job assigned during this week of torture and then rest when they can. The other group are called "Optimizers," those who imagine all the tasks lined up for them during the day and think about how much time and effort they should put into each.

One group does better than the other. If you had to guess, which would you say drop out more often: Taskers or Optimizers?

McGrath told us, "The people who drop out are overwhelmingly Optimizers. They focus on the big picture; and they don't rest because they are always thinking about the next thing they have to do. The secret of success for the Taskers is they take this monolithic thing and break it into chunks. It's task, rest. Task, rest."

As the saying goes, you don't try to eat an elephant all at once; you have to divide it into easily digestible parts. This chunking tactic is also used by athletes. "You'll see many ultramarathoners and triathletes doing this. They focus on the next immediate objective—the next point on the horizon—and prevent their minds from passing to the entire race," writes Charles Chu in his newsletter the *Open Circle*.

The point for leaders: Many of our employees are feeling overloaded with crushing amounts of work to accomplish, and it's leading to unprecedented levels of stress and anxiety. A first tactic any manager can try is to help team members break down their work into optimal chunks. Of course, this is only one of a number of methods of helping lessen the mental weight of workloads. In this chapter, we'll explore those tactics and how they may be best implemented to reduce anxiety levels and build resilience in team members. But first, it's important to address a few widespread misconceptions about overload.

They Just Can't Keep Up (and Other Common Myths)

Most common of the myths of overload: Many managers believe it is an individual failure, thinking, *Oh, he just can't keep up.* Consider that in the US alone, research in 2019 from global staffing firm Robert Half showed 91 percent of employees felt at least somewhat burned out at that moment, defined as mentally and physically exhausted from work. That's a clear indication that the problem is more macro than micro.

Some managers argue it is a lack of resiliency that's at the core of this issue. Yet some of the most resilient of all workers experience burnout in high numbers. Take the case of healthcare professionals. As Adam Grant of the Wharton School reported in the *New York Times*, "More than half of doctors and a third of nurses regularly feel burned out," and that was before the COVID-19 crisis. As their dedication to their work during the outbreak admirably demonstrated, battling through long days in hellish conditions, these are among the most resilient people on the planet. Adrienne Boissy, MD, chief experience officer at the renowned Cleveland Clinic, makes the point forcefully. "I held three jobs in college, completed a residency for four years, and this was followed by two years of fellowship. I completed a master's degree in bioethics and became a staff neurologist. During that time, I moved multiple times, said goodbye to many relationships, and missed key events in the lives of my friends and family because I was working." She summed up: "Resilience—the very idea that you're able to recover or bounce back from hardship— is *required* to become a clinician. The path itself selects individuals who can navigate and tolerate the challenges it produces."

Boissy is mystified why most of the approaches that businesses take to helping people cope with crushing workloads are aimed at "fixing" the person, such as offering meditation and yoga classes, or tips for getting good sleep, healthy eating, and getting organized. While those can be effective ways to reduce stress and alleviate anxiety, they ignore a core problem: Organizations are hiring fewer staff members to do the work and raising stress to unhealthy levels. The result: It's impossible to keep up.

Focusing on just the individual diverts attention from fixing underlying issues with the amount of work assigned and the ways in which employees are managed and are expected to do their jobs, not to mention the clear fact that there needs to be a more realistic accounting of how many people are actually needed to accomplish tasks.

Stress as a Tool

Another misconception we commonly hear is that overload is good for productivity. In the short term, for crunch situations, that actually can be true. The human body responds to stress by burning fuel to release energy, and that can give us a burst of speed to respond to immediate threats. But crunch time has become the standard, causing excessive pressure on team members. And research shows chronic stress causes wear and tear to our bodies, increasing the risk of developing anxiety as well as age-related diseases such as cancer, diabetes, and dementia.

Consider the experience of an executive coaching client of ours, Quan, who is a midlevel manager at a technology company. In our first session, he bemoaned his situation: "My team worked sixteen-hour days to update our SAP system. We took it as a source of pride to accomplish the upgrade faster than any team before." A problem arose, however. After leaders saw that Quan's team had met this incredibly accelerated schedule, it became the new standard. "Now," he said, "the company expects the next upgrade in a 10 percent shorter timeframe, and that really is impossible. I made a mistake in pushing my team so hard on the last upgrade."

Leaders often fail to appreciate that constantly demanding more and more work in less and less time will inevitably lead to employee frustration and distrust, rising anger levels, and eventually, for countless employees, burnout. Yet team managers often tell us they don't have time to help their people with overload since they are underwater themselves. "They just have to learn to buck up" is a common refrain we hear. But bosses who fail to appreciate the effects of an excessive load on their team members are likely to worsen the situation and can be blind to the corrosive effects of overload on team performance. Offering only palliatives like relaxation methods—temporarily helpful though they may be—may actually make their employees more anxious and more ticked off.

The effects of overload are causing companies a staggering amount of lost work time, turnover, and health-care expenses. Employees who report being burned out are 63 percent more likely to take sick time and 2.6 times as likely to leave their current employer, according to a Gallup survey. Meanwhile, the psychological and physical problems of burned-out employees account for up to $190 billion a year in health-care spending in the US alone, according to Bain & Company. Helping employees cope before they burn out, or shove off for another job, is therefore a great productivity booster.

Hiding in Plain Sight

A final misunderstanding to mention is that some managers tell us their employees won't admit they are about to burn out. Team members try to cover up their growing anxiety, so how is a boss supposed to know if there's a problem relating to individual overload? Well, that is the duck syndrome at work. But it's all the more reason that managers need to be proactive in addressing the problem. Allowing overload to escalate into anxiety and burnout can have negative ricocheting effects on an entire work group. Harvard psychologist Harry Levinson listed as symptoms of burnout at work: chronic fatigue and self-criticism for putting up with the demands; anger at those putting the burdens on you; cynicism, negativity, and irritability; and a sense of being besieged. None of that is good for team spirit. Even one employee feeling this can bring down the morale of an entire work group in the time it takes to grumble, "You'll never believe what they want me to do *now*."

The sad fact is that in too many companies, unrealistic amounts of work are assigned with unrealistic deadlines. Managers often tell us there isn't much they can do about that; they aren't the ones setting those big goals. And yet we find it *is* often possible to bring the work assigned to a team considerably more in line with what's realistically manageable. Sometimes this can come when a manager makes a compelling case in negotiations with top leaders, or if that fails, by pitching to hire additional staff or short-term contractors. It can also come by reducing excessive red tape.

We've seen this as a major issue in the overload of workers in health care. If you want to hear a medical professional curse, ask them how many hours they waste a year entering every detail imaginable into a patient's electronic health record, or the forms they have to fill out to renew their medical licenses, hospital privileges, drug-prescribing authority, and so on. Even before the COVID-19 crisis, the risk of burnout in this profession was acute. We've found one of the best ways health-care organizations are helping their staff to gain control over exhaustion is to change the situation that is causing it—reducing digital demands.

There are typically things all managers can do to reduce red tape, which can be remarkably empowering for their team members; for instance, conducting formal kaizen events with company approval to streamline processes in their team or assigning necessary paperwork to a person who likes doing it (which suggests the need to get to know what employees are motivated by).

While Job One for a leader is doing whatever is possible to bring workloads into alignment with realistic expectations for productivity, we appreciate that in many cases making substantial changes to workload simply is not feasible. If by this point you are thinking that this just isn't going to work in your firm, then we offer below a set of methods for helping your people better cope with workload expectations.

Method 1: Create Clear Roadmaps

One way to help reduce employee anxiety regarding overload is to decide upon clear, achievable goals for everyone on the team. Yet rather than this being a top-down doling out of assignments, we've found more leaders are doing this collaboratively with feedback from their people.

It is rare for us to find team members working from good, understandable roadmaps that can be referred to again and again, providing clarity on what needs to get done in what timeframe (week/month/year). Yet in an interview with Mary Beth DeNooyer, chief human resources officer for Keurig Dr Pepper, she said their twenty thousand employees operate daily from personalized frameworks that provide clarity and help reduce anxiety. In addition to specific individual work goals and targets on these roadmaps, "they include our Vision: What are we trying to achieve from a macro perspective," she said. "We also include Company Values, how our teams work together; and Competencies, which are how an individual succeeds."

DeNooyer said the frameworks are an anchor that employees can refer back to, helping them prioritize and avoid frustration. "People have them hanging on their bulletin board or as a screensaver," she added. "And when the world seems to be on fire, they can lean back and say, 'Okay, does this new thing fit?' If not, they probably don't need to be working on it."

As a new step in creating roadmaps, involving the entire group in the process of developing team targets is powerful for a few key reasons. First, team members are better than bosses at knowing how much time particular tasks will take, and what impediments they may hit to getting them done; and when a manager really listens to this input it helps reduce unnecessary stress going forward. Second, by working transparently as a group, everyone can understand and align on the most critical priorities for the team as a whole. Third, research has shown that giving teams a greater sense of control over their collective goals is a boon for engagement and productivity. We've known this for some time. For instance, in 1939, Kurt Lewin conducted what we believe is the first study to identify if group expectations would strengthen achievement at the Harwood Pajama Factory in Virginia. Several teams of workers at the factory were given a chance to set their own goals, and the participants met for thirty minutes each week to talk about challenges they were facing and collectively discuss whether they were ready to increase productivity or keep it the same.

During the weekly meetings, it became clear that workers were using different methods to accomplish the same tasks on the line, which led to improvements and standardizations in processes that enhanced productivity. At the end of each meeting, the group voted on whether to increase their daily output, to what level, and over what period of time. As a result, they eventually voted to enhance output from seventy-five units an hour to eighty-seven over a period of five days. A few weeks later, they agreed they could increase output again. Throughout the next five months, the group maintained its growth and achieved output well beyond anything seen before. Lewin believed that this democratic way of decision-making was the key to productivity growth. In fact, groups tested later—that had no democratic voting, and where a manager set the goals—did not achieve anywhere near the same productivity growth.

We find a collaborative goal-setting process like this can also build team spirit. As Adam Goodman, director of the Center for Leadership at Northwestern University, writes, "Working toward something together, that you're committed to, forms strong bonds and fosters collaboration." Open, mutual discussions like Lewin observed with team members help create a sense of shared vision; and according to our research, employees are much less likely to burn out when they can easily see the connection between their work and their team's or organization's larger mission and vision in a way that makes them feel that their job is vital and that the work they are doing is making a real difference.

Method 2: Balance Loads

As part of the collaborative roadmap process we just described, it's essential to ensure that workloads are well-balanced among team members to avoid certain members becoming overwhelmed. In many teams we visit, we find a handful of stressed-out workhorses putting in seventy-hour weeks while other employees appear happy-go-lucky, heading home at five every day.

How can a manager ensure everyone on the team has the right amount of work?

DeNooyer of Keurig Dr Pepper adds that she monitors her team's workload regularly and tries to create an environment where team members help each other during peak times to ensure no one gets overloaded too often. "I have weekly touchpoints with my team, and when I can tell that it's getting too much, I'll say, 'Okay, what's the list of things? And which ones do you *have* to do? Which ones can be shared with somebody else? Which ones can wait?'" By balancing in this way, she is methodical about setting priorities for the coming week, and is transparent about what trade-offs must be made, projects that can be delayed, and who else they might need to get involved.

With this, we know some anxious employees are driven intrinsically to impress and take on more and more, and managers can tend to over-rely on these people because they are so willing. These folks end up doing disproportionately heavy lifting until it becomes too much. Yet it's dangerous to conflate hours worked with productivity, as that can create more anxiety in the team. Hours and results are not the same thing. Some employees can get an incredible amount done in a typical workday and head out at five, and there's nothing wrong with that.

"It's important to make sure your employees understand you don't equate hours with productivity," says Liane Davey, cofounder of 3COze Inc. The best way to do this, she says, is to openly praise strong performance, irrespective of hours worked. "If José put up great numbers last week—even if he leaves at 4:30 every day—you need to celebrate him in a public forum. If people complain [about his hours] or you pick up on gossip, head it off at the pass. Say, 'I encourage you to pay attention to what people are accomplishing and contributing as opposed to the sheer number of hours they work.'"

Reallocating work and dispersing tasks among team

members takes time and effort, typically several hours in a manager's week. It involves thinking critically about who is getting overloaded, who is motivated by what, who needs an opportunity to develop, and what our priorities are right now. Achieving balance is never easy, and never perfect. It's inevitable that at any given time, a few people will be doing a disproportionate amount of work. But the key is to ensure that no one person is overloaded all the time. That kind of effort on the part of a manager can greatly reduce stress levels for everyone.

Kyle Arteaga, CEO of The Bulleit Group, points to one example from early in his career when he headed up a team at Reuters. He managed a star performer named Janice. A high-profile and interesting assignment arose, and Arteaga's impulse was to hand it to Janice. Before, however, he had a candid one-on-one with her to find out what was currently on her plate and if she could handle this new project. "I also encouraged her to talk to her clients and team members to determine if this additional work would fit into her schedule."

Janice was able to take on the extra work, but Arteaga helped her be strategic about other tasks that came her way after to avoid pushing her too far toward burnout. "Sometimes, she would purposefully put herself on the bench to wait for a better opportunity around the corner," he said. "I helped her assess opportunities."

This process is made easier by having team members participate in setting the balance as part of a team effort. Admittedly this can be tricky. If you asked a random group of employees, most will tell you they are pulling their own weight, and then some. Typically, the ones who will agree to take on additional assignments are the Janices—those who are already carrying more than their fair share. It's also true that few employees will want to inconvenience their fellow teammates by dumping their work on them.

Yet we have found that teams can work together very effectively when everyone engages in regular load-balancing discussions. During the meetings, managers typically should assume the role of facilitator (guiding the discussion and ensuring everyone is involved) or assign someone to the role who can effectively run the meeting. At a minimum, the team leader should have all possible facts and figures at hand to help adjudicate and make workloads fairer (e.g., *Todd took on the last two new projects, let's give someone else a turn*, or *Sarah, you just ended your assignment with IT, do you have bandwidth now?*). Another key member of the meeting is the Promise Tracker, someone who makes a list of who agrees to what and the timelines.

We found a good example of team load-balancing when we worked with a biotech firm. A leader of a quality team had called such a meeting during a crisis in the factory: A contaminant had been found in one of their sterile products. During the meeting, a senior staff member mentioned they could postpone their deviation reports for up to thirty days and still meet FDA requirements. The reports document exceptions found to normal operating procedures, and the team normally prided themselves on completing them within days.

Decision made, the team was then able to prioritize the next few weeks' efforts on finding the point of contamination.

The quality team got through the crisis and found it helpful to continue to meet weekly thereafter to balance loads, which resulted in the streamlining of several of their key processes. They discovered some work they'd been doing for years could be safely omitted entirely—for instance, one batch report was no longer required at all by regulators, and an internal audit that had been conducted monthly could be done quarterly. Left to work individually, the team members would most likely never have come up with these solutions. Tensions would have mounted, and goals might have been missed. Instead, conditions improved for everyone.

Method 3: Rotate People

If it's possible given the nature of their business, leaders should consider moving people out of high-load and high-stress jobs into lower-stress ones in a rotating schedule to avoid anxiety overload. "Changes of pace, changes of demands, and shifts into situations that may not be so draining enable people to replenish their energies and get new and more accurate perspectives on themselves and their roles," counseled Harvard's Harry Levinson. Change also helps people be able to look forward to a time when they can get out of tough assignments.

A study among nurses in the United States found job rotation helped reduce burnout. It also inspired staff members to achieve higher performance and allowed them to gain new knowledge and skills. Best of all for their hospitals, it increased the quality of care given to patients.

A practitioner of job rotating is Matthew Ross, co-owner of The Slumber Yard, an online mattress review firm. His goal with moving people between jobs has been to enhance employee satisfaction, reduce turnover, and have his team members gain valuable new skills. Employees transfer to other lateral jobs as often as quarterly, and he finds that training employees to be competent in multiple disciplines helps reduce stress when one of them has to fill in for a colleague who's out for a day or if an employee moves on.

When done thoughtfully and with proper training, rotating jobs can also be an opportunity to help people move out of their comfort zones and work in areas where they may not normally be assigned. It's also a chance to consider a person's core motivators, to find work that will give them a greater sense of satisfaction.

We conducted a job rotation exercise with our team and ended up shifting bookkeeping duties, which Adrian had been doing as one of the owners. The role was happily assumed by a team member who loved detail-oriented logistics. In short order, she became much better at the job than Adrian had ever been. She also appreciated the role, as it gave her a chance to learn, grow, and flex her analytical muscles.

Method 4: Closely Monitor Progress
An important next step to build resilience is to check in frequently with one's team about how they are holding up, as

a group and individually. A laissez-faire management approach rarely works—relying on the annual performance review as the only check-in, for instance—but neither does micromanaging people and leaving them feeling as if they're watched over by "Big Brother" (the Orwellian type, not the CBS reality show). The sweet spot is in the middle, and if done correctly, employees greatly appreciate it.

Rather than viewing check-ins as wielding a stick, see it as a way to allow team members to share challenges that are developing in a timely fashion, so that you can work together to find solutions. As Jamie Dimon, CEO of JPMorgan Chase, tells his team, "If there is a problem and you tell me, it's *our* problem. If there's a problem and you don't tell me, it's *your* problem." It bears repeating that sometimes all an employee needs is a sympathetic ear to bend when he has an issue; other times he'll need advice and intervention.

Another highly successful senior executive offered similar advice on sharing challenges to her team. Shelly Lazarus, chairman emeritus of Ogilvy & Mather, once told us leaders should tell their team members: "If you are not going to hit a goal, please let me know earlier rather than later." She reflected that, in too many companies, "we go through monthly meetings where people don't fess up and admit: 'I'm not going to make that number.' The reason they don't is that they think they are going to be punished. Rather than punishing them at that point, you should laud them in front of others and thank them for their honesty and for giving us the time to make the adjustments by the end of the year." Rewarding those who ask for help is critical, she concluded. "Let them know it is excellent behavior."

Team check-ins might be done in regular staff meetings or in special update meetings. The goal is to ensure that all team members are on the same page as time progresses by asking questions such as: What fresh obstacles are we facing to hitting our team targets, what will we not be able to deliver on time if things keep going as they are, what are we hearing from the client, who on the team is held up waiting for what deliverables, and who needs help?

As to individual check-ins, anxiety can be allayed when leaders regularly ask employees about their workloads privately. Let's face it, some people will never be comfortable talking about feeling overloaded in a team setting. A particular issue to be aware of is that new hires and younger workers are often more reticent to ask for help, for various reasons. They're afraid of being a burden. They want to look capable. For many, they're used to being able to do all their work on their own (as with their college course load). Their lack of familiarity with many aspects of business procedures can be daunting or frustrating.

It's important to tell your people that you see asking for help as a sign of strength rather than weakness. Also let every employee know that you're asking the entire team about how they're managing their loads in individual meetings; that way they won't feel singled out. You want to be sure that in asking, you convey that you're doing so in order to solve problems where you can. Then it's important to follow up to do just that.

To lessen anxiety, we've found some good questions to ask in these individual check-ins include:

+ Do you feel like you can complete the project by deadline without having to work unreasonable hours?

+ Is there anyone else on the team who could help so you could meet the deadline?

+ Is there any part of this project that might be delayed?

+ Do you need any additional training or resources to be successful?

+ What have you learned that we might do differently next time we are up against a task like this?

Of course, wrenches can be thrown into the works at any moment that will require emergency one-on-ones. That's why the best leaders we see keep an open-door policy as much as possible, making sure their team members know they are really okay with them coming in to talk about issues or ask questions. Naturally there are times leaders have to restrict access, but too often in our surveys we hear employees complain something to the effect of, "My boss comes in at nine and leaves at six, but I have no idea what he's doing all day. I don't see him, and he's never around when I need help." An open door means limiting meetings as much as possible and announcing to your team times every day that are "office hours." Keep in mind that according to a Gallup report, employees who have a manager who's willing to listen to their work-related problems are 62 percent less likely to be burned out.

Method 5: Help People Prioritize

We have found that too often, employees are left to figure out entirely on their own how to prioritize their work, and that can be an anxiety accelerator. Even a quick discussion with a boss, or with colleagues, would be a great assist.

At first, this can be a daily custom with a manager and new employee, not to be overly controlling but to offer help and guidance as they get settled. Managers may ask each morning: *What do you have going on today? Okay, let's now organize those tasks by level of priority to the team.* We recommend using clear criteria to grade the work to be done, such as Critical, Important, Moderate, and Low, and then to link each project to a business need. Manager and employee can then discuss what might be able to wait until tomorrow. In this way, less experienced people can learn to bite off chunks of the elephant every day and feel good about their accomplishments.

As employees get more experience, a boss may move this sort of prioritization planning to a weekly or even monthly process. Project management software can help as well, ensuring goals and timelines are available for everyone to see.

Dr. Rita McGrath of Columbia Business School offered a metaphor for prioritizing: "Your day is a truck, and each hour is a box on the truck. When someone delegates to you, you have to be clear to them that a box will have to come off the truck to fit the new one. There are consequences. When it comes to overload, we are not terrific at articulating to each other what our priorities are and what we are working on."

This can especially ratchet up anxiety for lower-power people, underrepresented minorities, and younger workers. "It's almost a disloyal thing to say I'm really overloaded, and this will push me over the edge," said Dr. McGrath. "It's important for managers to make it okay to have that dialogue. And for leaders to remember that the more senior they are, the more their suggestions are commands."

McGrath recalls being a PhD student at Wharton. She was busy running a research center, managing undergrads, and completing her own studies, all while commuting an hour each way and raising two kids under the age of four. "I showed up one day and the head of our center introduced me to a visiting scholar from Singapore. He wanted me to escort the professor around for the day. I asked for a word in the next room, and I told him that if he thought that was the best use of my time, I'd do it; but I made him aware of all the things that would not get done that day. His eyes got wide and he admitted he had no idea."

McGrath had the courage to speak up to her department chair and have an open dialogue about priorities because trust existed in the relationship.

Method 6: Avoid Distractions

In a series of experiments conducted by PhDs Joshua Rubinstein, a researcher at the Federal Aviation Administration, and Jeffrey Evans and David Meyer of the University of Michigan, test subjects were required to switch between different tasks, such as solving math problems. No surprise, the participants lost time when they had to move back and forth from one job to another. As tasks got more complex, participants lost more and more time trying to get back up to speed. As a result, the multitaskers were significantly slower at accomplishing the overall set of assignments than control groups that completed one task then moved on to the next. The research, published in the *Journal of Experimental Psychology*, found productivity decreased by as much as 40 percent when test subjects were repeatedly switching tasks.

A University of London study shows that workers who are distracted by incoming emails and telephone calls drop ten points on IQ scores on average. And yet more than half of the 1,100 people surveyed said they responded to emails immediately or as soon as possible, with 21 percent admitting they would interrupt an in-person meeting to respond to a text or other electronic missive. Lead researcher Dr. Glenn Wilson said that such unchecked infomania can reduce workers' mental sharpness. "Those who are constantly breaking away from tasks to react to email or text messages suffer similar effects on the mind as losing a night's sleep," he said.

One of the traits we've noted in high-performing people is their remarkable ability to reduce distractions and calmly concentrate on one subject at a time. In the biography *Abraham Lincoln*, Carl Sandburg shared a story of a young Lincoln. An observer noted the president-to-be sitting on a log, lost in thought, wrestling with a vexing issue. Hours later, Lincoln was in the same position. Finally, a light broke across his face and he returned to his law office. Lincoln had the ability to sit with a problem long enough that it surrendered its secrets to him. Today, we find encouraging even a few minutes of solitude—to take a walk or listen to music—can allow employees to better tackle challenges and get their work done more efficiently and more calmly.

We found a terrific example of how one manager was helping reduce distractions in Kim Cochran, regional sales manager for Fluke Industrial Group, a manufacturer of electronic test tools and software. Cochran is the sales leader of a nine-state region, and when she came on board the company was losing many of its valuable technical salespeople. By the time we interviewed her, three years later, Cochran hadn't lost a single one.

She says much of that success was the result of eliminating distractions so her team members could focus on what they enjoy doing—making sales and supporting clients. Her people are all remote, and they travel every day, so her goal was to help them feel included and listened to, but never overwhelmed by information. As such, she classifies all email messages that come in from corporate on a ladder—from least urgent to most:

- On the lowest rung are things that she can take care of for her direct reports without bothering them. *Boom, done.*

- The next rung up involves Important information that does need her employees' attention but isn't going to make or break their sales efforts—due dates for benefits sign-ups, deadlines for sales forecasts, and so on. She cuts the messages down to the core information and sends these in a short email (with a link to more information if they want it). Her people know she tries to screen information, so an email from Cochran is going to be important.

- Next up the ladder is information she classifies as Hot Topics, those items that her folks will need to give serious attention. This may be changes in their work process, organizational structure, pay plan, pricing, and so on. During the week she compiles these on a running agenda and brings them up one-by-one in a weekly open-forum call with the entire team, answering questions and promising to take concerns back to senior leadership.

- The top step on her ladder is information classified as Urgent—those 911 items that can't wait even a day. In this case, Cochran schedules a huddle phone call at day's end, when most of her people are available. But she does this sparingly and only for true emergencies.

Of course, Cochran's strategy is not the only way of cutting down on interruptions. Some managers we've worked with have developed ticketing systems to manage workflow; others encourage their team members to clearly review the work they already have going with clients when they are approached with new jobs—to help create realistic expectations and avoid overload.

Method 7: Encourage R&R

Leading researchers have stressed the importance of quality downtime for workers. "People need to take time off to recharge. Not only do they need to have time when they're not working, but they need to have time when they're not *thinking* about work," says Dr. David Ballard, head of the Psychologically Healthy Workplace Program at the American Psychological Association.

Ryan Westwood, CEO of Simplus, told us leaders must be more thoughtful about when they message their team members. "I got an email from my boss once on a Sunday morning. And that's a day when I like to be with my family and take a collective sigh of relief and do other things that aren't work-related. It ruined my whole day; it created anxiety for me.

"Most employees care what their boss cares about, and it will be on their minds even if they aren't supposed to respond. It's much easier to set the timer on your email to let it drop Monday morning at eight. We need to give our people time to spend doing things not work-related so that they're ready for their workweek."

Managers should also encourage their people to use their vacation time and be an example themselves by taking time to unwind—and then telling stories about what they did away from the office. And they can realize that part of R&R may happen on work time. More than 70 percent of employees report increased productivity when they take short breaks during the day to exercise, socialize, or just grab a breath of fresh air.

In this always-on world, and with many of us now living in our offices, it's important for managers to help their people rest and get away as much as possible.

*   *   *

As the intensity of the COVID-19 pandemic became clear in 2020, a positive mantra was shared around the world: "We're in this together!" In helping employees cope with overload, that is a message that bears repeating regularly. By taking the steps we've outlined in this chapter, you'll make sure your people know that when you say, "We are in this together," you really mean it, and they will in turn help one another lift their loads.

We've seen teams working together in that way, and they're not only the most productive, but the most personally rewarding work groups for managers to lead.

Help with Overload

- Leaders often fail to appreciate that constantly demanding more and more work in less and less time will lead to employee frustration, rising anger levels, and eventually anxiety and burnout.

- Managers may believe it is an individual failure when an employee is overwhelmed, and yet more than 90 percent of employees feel burned out at least some of the time. The problem is often organizational.

- Most approaches businesses take to helping people cope with crushing workloads are aimed at fixing the person instead of focusing on underlying issues with the amount of work assigned and with the ways in which employees are managed.

- When employees feel anxiety from overload, managers can start by helping them break work into optimal chunks.

- Other methods to help team members better cope with workload expectations and reduce anxiety levels include: 1) create clear roadmaps, 2) balance loads, 3) rotate people, 4) closely monitor progress, 5) help people prioritize, 6) avoid distractions, and 7) encourage R&R.

SUMMARY

Clear Paths Forward

HELP TEAM MEMBERS
CHART THEIR WAY

—

Leadership is about making others better as a result of your presence and making sure that impact lasts in your absence.

—Sheryl Sandberg, chief operating officer, Facebook

A great deal of study has been done about one domain of online life and the link to anxiety: social media. The research spotlights that as people constantly peer into what others are up to online, they are often led to feel unsettled about their own lives: Are they doing as many fun things, traveling to as many cool places, and doing as well? Few things create more unhappiness in human beings than comparing ourselves to others.

When it comes to work, we are seeing similar FOMO worries. Workers, especially younger ones, can become concerned that by staying put in a job, they might miss out on something more interesting, more secure, or more lucrative. We believe the effects of the rising generation growing up as "digital natives" goes some way to explain an issue we hear from managers: Young employees are more anxious about their jobs.

In the online world, the formula for success is proven. You post, get likes, add followers, and repeat. And it's a fast-working formula. In contrast, young people often find the corporate world excruciatingly slow and frustrating. They are eager to be given promotions, be trusted with added responsibility, and receive raises, but they don't want to pay their dues, boss after boss tells us.

Typically, younger workers *are* more antsy about moving up or moving on. The research bears it out. While 40 percent of boomers stayed with an employer for at least twenty years, and one in five stayed for thirty years or more, relatively content to climb the corporate ladder in the company's own due time, 78 percent of Gen Zers and 43 percent of millennials surveyed in 2018 planned to leave their companies within two years to pursue greener pastures. Yet leaders must understand that all this job hopping is not just about a fear of missing out or a desire to get promoted, it's also about wage stagnation. Entry-level jobs, especially in urban areas, do not pay salaries that enable young people to build lives. According to Brookings Institution data, 44 percent of all workers qualified as "low wage" earners in 2019. Their median hourly wages were $10.22 an hour, with annual earnings of about $18,000.

In short, said Brookings, "there aren't enough good jobs to go around," and young people are well aware of it.

The fact is, most of us measure ourselves by hitting life markers: graduating from high school, attending college/ starting an apprenticeship, getting a decent job, marrying, buying a home, having children, and so on. Society tends to think of these milestones as events that "settle" people. But access to these markers has changed for the rising generations. The average age to get on the housing ladder now is well over thirty. Add bloated student loans, lower wages, and fewer high-paying opportunities, and many of the things that society considers part of "normal adult life" can feel a long way off, if not unattainable. Instead of midlife crises, we are now seeing what we call the "quarter-life crisis," where those in their twenties are facing serious unrest about the quality and direction of their lives.

One young worker spoke for her generation when she told us, "We no longer see companies as having our best interests in mind. We understand that shareholder value is king, and we can be replaced by cheaper labor." This is why, according to a 2018 study by ManpowerGroup, 87 percent of millennials ranked job security as a top priority (more than likely to be even more important in the post-pandemic world).

All this may also help explain why so many young workers are concerned with gaining new skills in their jobs. A Gallup poll of millennials found 87 percent "highly value" growth and development opportunities—almost 20 percent higher than Gen X and boomer workers. Sadly, the same poll found that only 39 percent of young employees felt that they had "learned something new on the job in the past month." Helping people develop new skills can be a terrific opportunity for enlightened managers to keep and engage their workforce. Research by Deloitte has found that organizations that effectively nurture their people's desire to learn are at least 30 percent more likely to be market leaders in their industries.

While the phenomenon of career anxiety may seem a massive societal shift that managers might not have a lot of control over, in fact, there is a great deal they can do. We agree with J. Maureen Henderson of *Forbes*, who cautions leaders not to simply resign themselves to millennial "high turnover and short staff tenures rather than [focus] on retaining their existing employees." Indeed, we have found that when leaders offer younger workers regular chances to learn and advance—and find ways to help secure their futures within an organization—many of those valuable employees prefer to stay.

If leaders are seeking to retain the best young workers, and reduce unnecessary career anxiety in their people, then addressing concerns about job security, growth, and advancement are vital. This is a terrific way for leaders and their firms to stand out in a competitive job market. According to Corporate Executive Board research, only one in ten organizations have what can be defined as a learning culture: a workplace that supports organizational and independent quests for knowledge that will advance the company's mission (not to mention make workers more skilled and add more value).

We understand that for a busy manager—and is there any other kind?—the notion of closely shepherding each person's career development may seem overwhelming. But it doesn't have to be burdensome. Following the methods we outline here will not only address your employees' anxiety about where they're heading, it will relieve the tension you feel about their worries and demands.

Method 1: Create More Steps to Grow

More than 75 percent of Gen Z workers say they believed they should be promoted within their first year on the job. If it's possible to implement, one highly effective means of alleviating employee anxiety about advancing is simply to create more steps on the promotional ladder. This was done to great effect at the appropriately named Ladders, an online job search website. The company's founder and CEO, Marc Cenedella, said of his tech-savvy young workers, when they "arrived at my company, they fussed over promotions, pay, and responsibilities. They demanded work far out of line with what their capabilities and experiences qualified them for."

At the time, Ladders had a program that enabled a new hire to be promoted to senior associate within two years. "To our Gen X way of thinking, this was way fairer than what the baby boomers put us through," he said. But the young workers coming in perceived it as a slow passing of years with nothing to show for it on their resumes.

Cenedella admits that, at first, he tried badgering younger colleagues into seeing things his way. But eventually he realized he'd have better results by adapting his own point of view. He revised the program to provide six promotions over two years—with performance hurdles, title increases, and pay bumps every step of the way. "We kept the same performance standards, the same final pay rate, and the same progression toward expertise over time," he says. "We learned that more frequent career feedback, with better chances for getting ahead, and some self-direction were actually very effective tools for building morale and contributing to the success of our company."

Sadly, providing a reassuring sense of achievement like this comes off like delusional coddling to some managers we've discussed the process with (ironically, many of the same people who helped raise the new generation). So, we share the results Ladders has seen. Cenedella said new hires have worked hard to reach each new level and take every promotion seriously. When, after just four months, they move from junior analyst to analyst, they celebrate, call Mom and Dad, and share fist bumps with team members. Leaders quickly realized the moves weren't being seen by employees as fake promotions but were significant signposts of success on their career journey. And thanks to a focus on mastering specific levels of accomplishment before moving to each promotion, Cenedella also says Ladders now boasts a more capable and focused workforce for new hires of every age.

Many managers who've implemented similar steps in promotion have told us it's great not only for employee engagement but for training. It provides more opportunities for manager-employee coaching, and also facilitates richer discussions with people about their big-picture development goals.

Method 2: Coach Employees about How to Get Ahead

For many employees who experience anxiety about advancing in their careers, we find it's due in part to a lack of understanding about the best tactics for standing out as a candidate for promotion. Managers can open employees' eyes to the ways in which they can take charge of their own career development, including adding new skills, gaining experience, and producing the kind of results that senior leaders will care about, which will make them more qualified for moving up.

Dr. David B. Peterson, former director of executive coaching and development at Google, stressed to us that many employees don't understand that they've got to invest quality time every week in preparing to take on future roles. Too many employees are focused only on optimizing their performance in their current role, which, of course, is something every manager wants every employee to do. But a focus too exclusively on pleasing one's current boss, without looking ahead and planning for growth into new challenges, leaves people feeling at the mercy of just the one person they report to. That can exacerbate anxiety, as years can pass without even a hint of moving up.

Peterson says, "Leaders need to help team members figure out that just being excellent in their current role is not going to get them where they want to go. What will get them to the next level are new and different skills." He advises managers to take their team members through something he calls the "reality test," looking back a week and then ahead a week at their calendars to see how much of their time is spent on tasks that will help get them where they want to be a year from now. Do their daily actions align with their expressed goals? Obviously the bulk of a person's time will be spent on current tasks, but if little to no time is spent in learning and growing, there's little chance the person will ever move up.

So leaders can do a lot to help, allowing their people dedicated time each week—just an hour or two is a big start—to learn desirable skills and align their focus with their long-term personal development goals. This is a powerful way to help people feel supported. Of course, this implies that managers have met individually with all of their employees to understand their career goals and how they might help them get where they want to go.

Method 3: Help Employees Assess Their Skills and Motivations

Another part of coaching, and helping tamp down anxiety about the path forward, is helping employees gain clarity about the path they'd actually most like to travel, which many employees are unsure of. Indecision can lead to career stress, and taking the wrong path can move people into roles they're neither well-suited for nor very interested in—just because they think they need to keep moving up.

Not long ago, we coached a department director about some possible pitfalls if she promoted Greg, one of her employees. The director was about to be moved to another role and had been grooming Greg to take her place. We assessed her team using our Motivators Assessment and conducted 360 interviews, and we believed that Greg was not likely to find her management job satisfying or be especially good at it.

As background, we built the Motivators Assessment with Drs. Travis Bradberry and Jean Greaves, authors of *Emotional Intelligence 2.0*, to help determine an individual's unique core drivers on the job. Twenty-three motivators emerged from our research that motivate people at work—from creativity to ownership, from money to learning. After having now surveyed more than 100,000 people with the Assessment, we've found a crucial element in employee engagement is for people to be authentically motivated by the work they're doing. Makes sense, right? The highest producing workers have a good quotient of work on their plates that's truly engaging for them.

Of course, all of us have aspects of our jobs we don't particularly enjoy. Everyone has to take out the trash, so to speak. But we've found managers can help employees become more committed, confident, and satisfied in their careers by helping them understand that while compensation and promotions are important, just as vital is doing something they're passionate about, with work they find interesting and rewarding. Employees who feel anxious about their career path may actually be on the wrong path. Caring managers can often help them know if that's the case, which we were hoping would happen in Greg's situation.

Discovering a mismatch between an employee's work and the kinds of tasks that would be more motivating also provides the opportunity to do some job sculpting with the employee: finding assignments they might *transfer* to someone else on the team, tasks that may be *altered* somewhat to become more motivating, and—best of all for the manager and employee—those things that they'll love doing may be *added* to a person's plate.

Rather than just giving employees promotions or raises (which can't be done very often), we've found this process of sitting down and sculpting their jobs can be powerful in increasing worker engagement and sense of direction. This is why we created the Motivators Assessment in the first place, to help leaders pinpoint what most engages their employees in their work. The assessment is now used by hundreds of organizations around the world to help managers better align their employees' jobs with core drivers, with well-documented results in performance and retention.

Coming back to the director and her employee Greg: We'd given this team the Motivators Assessment, and Greg's results showed that "Developing Others" and "Teamwork" were near the bottom of his list of twenty-three core drivers. That could be problematic. After all, if promoted, his new job would be about helping a department of a dozen people grow and "develop," all while building a cohesive group with a strong sense of "teamwork." We sat down and asked Greg to describe his *worst* days on the job, and he mentioned becoming frustrated when mentoring younger employees and/or helping one of his project teams work through sticky personnel issues and conflicts. When we asked Greg about his *best* days, he brightened up. He was usually off-site working with clients, solving their issues, and looking like a hero.

About people management, he confided, "My team members have conflicts. There are folks here who don't take feedback well. I have all these peers playing politics." Then he paused and asked, "You've done this awhile. Is that what management is always like?"

We nodded. "A lot of leading is just that. It's about resolving people issues, but it's also about enabling others to succeed." We added that some folks loved what he loathed.

Later we explained to Greg's boss that while he might become a serviceable manager, there was a very good chance he would be miserable in the role, which might lead to anxiety and burnout. It also might be clear, pretty fast, to his team members that his heart wasn't in the job.

We wish everyone always took our brilliant advice (or that our advice was always brilliant). This story took a turn for the worse. Based on the director's continued recommendation, after she was promoted to another role a few months later, Greg took over the team. He was smart, he'd figure it out, the company brass reasoned. That situation lasted for just about six months before the team revolted. Greg, they said, was slow to respond to their concerns, unsympathetic to their personal issues, and wrapped up in his own deliverables.

The HR partner assigned to his team had tried to coach Greg during the months he was in the role; but as sharp as Greg was, he just couldn't seem to change.

Thankfully, the company didn't fire him. The HR partner and Greg worked together to create a new role in which he would continue on the payroll as the team's senior consultant. In the three years since, he has taken on other tasks (internal executive coaching for one), broadened his reach working as a liaison with other departments, and assumed more responsibility in product development. Greg is a bright guy who, to the benefit of everyone involved, is no longer managing anyone except himself.

As this organization learned, putting people in the wrong positions can cause anxiety and undue stress, not only for the person in the wrong position, but also for the team they work with.

One last hard truth about this process is that sometimes coming to a clear understanding with an employee about the path they need to be on may lead to them leaving your team. And that might be optimal for the company and employee. That was the view of the CEO of a large insurance company we worked with.

We conducted motivation training for about a thousand leaders. Many were able to better align their daily tasks with their key drivers. As we sat down with the CEO to discuss the results, he told us three of his valued managers had decided to move on because of the training—one to become a teacher, another to open a small business, and the third to go back to university. We were a little nervous how he'd react, but he was just fine. "If they aren't happy, their employees are going to smell it on them," he said. "And to lose only three out of a thousand is pretty good. We have to be doing something right."

Like this CEO, good leaders aren't afraid to have their tribe members really consider what drives them at work—even if they may leave one day. A bonus is that this process can alleviate employee anxiety about advancement as well. And managers who help their employees learn what they'll be motivated by at work become known as great bosses to work for.

Bestselling author and former Oracle executive Liz Wiseman calls these leaders "talent magnets." She told us, "Smart, capable people find these bosses because of the reputation they build. They get known as the managers everyone wants to work for because of their ability to tap into people's native genius."

As Wiseman describes it, native genius is that thing you can do that makes you unique, a specific way your brain is wired that helps you add value—even if it may have been perceived as a negative in the past. She gave us a real-world example: Brian admitted he'd been called "Dr. No" in other places he'd worked. He couldn't help himself: He could immediately see flaws in any plan suggested by others. Instead of coaching Brian out of that habit, a talent magnet leader would work with it. She'd say, "Brian, this is great. Your native genius is finding potential pitfalls. What a terrific thing to have someone on the team who can find holes in our plans, who can look at the underbelly." While some managers might lament that Brian was a downer, a talent magnet would market his native genius to the team as a quality they needed. "We are going to use Brian whenever we are considering launching something major."

Adds Wiseman, this creates a real appreciation of diversity, and becomes incredibly engaging for the employee. "It's a pretty good gig when you can go to work and your boss and peers understand and appreciate your natural brilliance," she said. "And when a boss does that, she earns the right to say, 'You know, Brian, we also could use a little more from you here,' or 'I need you to do this differently.'"

The results for talent magnets can be astonishing, and they become widely recognized around a company. Ryan Westwood, CEO of Simplus, told us proudly of one of his employees: "He was in our marketing group as a graphic designer. He said he'd like to dip his toe into Salesforce consulting and get a certification. Two years later, he was the most certified person we had, with twenty-four, and he was considered one of the top one hundred Salesforce architects in the world. He became director of our solution department and started building intellectual property. All this because he was interested and ambitious and we opened up possibilities for him."

In contrast, one of Adrian's first jobs after earning his undergraduate degree was at a monthly magazine where he was hired as an editorial assistant. The promotion structure had been in place since the days of Gutenberg (it seemed). Editors were expected to remain in a role for about seven years, advancing like the march of a regimented clock from editorial assistant to assistant editor to associate editor. When he expressed interest in learning more and growing—he had an interest in leadership—Adrian was told the only opportunity for a higher-level job was to become the assistant managing editor, typically in your fifties, and then hope that the managing editor would quit or retire. He stayed only a short time and moved on to a company with actual opportunities, where those with ambition could aspire to follow their motivators.

To best understand what drives your people, we recommend having them take the Motivators Assessment, or at the very least take the time to observe and discuss what they seem to be most interested and engaged in at work. Again, this only happens when managers take the time to have more frequent assessments of skills and motivations with their people, and have honest discussions about what's realistic and what might not be.

Method 4: Use a Skill Development Flow

Part of reducing anxiety is teaching about potential growth upward, but we must also help employees understand that moving up isn't the only way to grow in a career. Says Mary Beth DeNooyer, chief human resources officer for Keurig Dr Pepper, "For a long time we thought about career paths as a ladder. It was all about how you move up. The imagery we're moving to is a rock wall, where a person can move up, sideways, a little up, and a little sideways. Everybody can have their own destination.

"The only thing you can't do on a rock wall is just hang there," she added. "You can't be content. You've got to move. But how you move and how fast and how high is up to you. That helps people think about what skills they are building. What they want to experience on their journey."

DeNooyer explains that a ladder implies one person climbs at a time; on a wall there can be many people who get to the same place without competing. In other words, success is not a zero-sum game. We've found this type of attitude can greatly enhance inclusion efforts and help alleviate the worries of some people who may feel threatened by diversity initiatives because they think spots are being taken away from them. Organizations that do this effectively create a culture where one person's growth doesn't have to come at the expense of someone else's.

When we coach leaders, we encourage them to follow a simple process to develop new skills in their team members. It follows our Skill Development Model. In using this method, leaders can help people trying to progress on the wall chart their own way. And, best of all, the process allows managers to align the company or team vision with the vision of their people, reducing anxiety that can arise if team members feel they aren't getting the growth they need.

First, either the employee suggests a skill to get better at, or the manager suggests it. If it's something that might benefit the team or organization, and the employee is on board to try, the employee begins to learn. If the skill is suggested by the employee and it's determined that it's not needed by

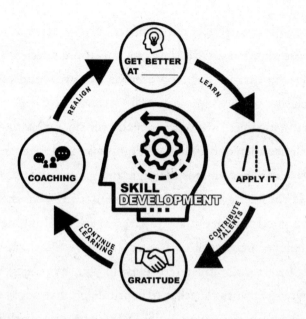

the organization at this time, then it might be something the worker would pursue on personal time. An employee of ours once said she wanted to become an audiologist working with children. While we thought it was a noble goal, we couldn't find a way to fit her training on that skill into our company needs. She ended up going to school in the evenings, and our support came in the form of giving her time off early a few days a week.

Next, after an employee starts to learn and acquires enough proficiency in the new skill to potentially help the team, a manager will find avenues to apply it. The employee will then contribute the new skill to helping the organization. Next, if the employee is making an effort and the skill is starting to make the team better, it's necessary for the manager to reward the behavior through gratitude and encourage continued learning. The manager will also provide coaching to ensure alignment with the company and team needs, and to offer any further help that's needed to grow and remove obstacles.

Finally, it comes time to realign and consider what's next. If the skill has been of benefit to the employee and the team, the employee may continue utilizing it and gaining more knowledge. If the manager or employee come to realize the skill is not a good fit, they may stop and try something new, or the employee may work on the skill on personal time. If the worker hasn't quite mastered the skill yet, the manager and employee may work together to continue progressing.

Anthony shared an example. When he was working at the University of Utah School of Medicine's Andrology and Epigenetics Research Lab, his leader Dr. Kenneth (Ki) Aston suggested Anthony's usefulness would be enhanced if he learned R programming, used to perform statistical data analysis. "I said I would try, but I wasn't confident," Anthony said. "Ki told me how valuable it could be for me. He set a goal and gave me the time and resources to learn. He also assigned one of the doctoral students to help me stumble through the learning process and understand how it all applied to the experiments we were running in the lab."

The doctoral student patiently watched as Anthony typed out code. "She could have input it in minutes; but if I had just watched her code, I wouldn't have learned. As I was typing, she would teach me, 'That part of the code tells the program to create categories, and this one labels the categories.' So I learned how the coding would affect other experiments.

"From there, she let me enter values and datapoints to really make sure I got a chance to master what she'd shown me. She never did the work for me, and she didn't expect me to be able to magically replicate what she did."

Within a few weeks, Anthony was proficient enough to help run analyses for several experiments. He acknowledges he could have been doing the wet bench work that he was brought in to tackle. He also could have run the analysis on Excel, a program he was familiar with. But his lab leader knew that R would be important for Anthony to learn as he expanded his progress as a scientist. After he had a foundational grasp of the language and was able to start contributing, Dr. Aston told him, "There's a lot more to learn on R, but this will do. Thanks for your contribution." And Anthony left the lab that day knowing that his efforts had been valued.

"I became even more dedicated to the lab after that. It made me feel like they cared about me ten times more," he said. "Developing a new skill made me feel like I was growing personally but also gaining stock and contributing to the lab's goals."

Method 5: Make Learning Real-Time

Want to see eyes glaze over or anxiety amp up? Mandate that busy employees attend a training session on "business writing skills," or "negotiating," or some such course that has little alignment to their day-to-day needs, says Steve Glaveski, CEO of Collective Campus in Melbourne, Australia.

Since the dawn of civilization when our ancestors first figured out how to use weapons to fight off pesky saber-toothed tigers, we humans have learned best when the learning is essential. (*Jeopardy* champ Ken Jennings may be the exception.) Matthieu Boisgontier of the University of British Columbia's Brain Behaviour Lab says, "Conserving energy has been essential for human survival, as it allowed us to be more efficient in searching for food and shelter, competing for sexual partners, and avoiding predators." Our brains are our bodies' biggest energy consumers, and for the sake of energy efficiency, they're designed to quickly forget information we don't need. After all, do you remember how to play a song on the recorder?

Of course, classes and virtual training in foundational business skills can be quite valuable, but the learning that will most excite employees, and make the most immediate impact on their performance, is about how to tackle the specific challenges they're facing in their work day-to-day.

Say one of your employees admits avoiding having a difficult, but necessary, conversation with a challenging colleague in another department she needs information from. She doesn't feel confident in knowing how to get a productive discussion going. You could walk her through an approach with some role-playing, providing her with language you might use. In addition, you could suggest she read the book *Crucial Conversations*, which is packed with gritty insights into dealing with troublesome colleagues. Steering employees toward literature you've found helpful, that is truly relevant, and that has pithy advice is a great way to foster their development (hey, as business book authors, we'd be horribly remiss not to endorse this practice).

Method 6: Tailor Development to the Individual

Having frequent and honest career-development conversations with employees allows managers to better discover the ways in which their people need to enhance their skills and are most interested in doing so. To reduce unnecessary anxiety, development should be tailored to individuals. This point was stressed to us by Dan Helfrich, CEO and Chairman of Deloitte Consulting. He's a terrific practitioner of a tailored approach, and it's won him the loyalty of his people, not to mention contributed to his promotion to a lofty position in his company.

Helfrich starts career one-on-ones by asking his direct reports: "What do you want to get better at?" This is so much more engaging for employees than being coached to fill skill gaps they have absolutely no interest in. Helfrich says, "I want to know about a challenge they feel ready to take on but haven't been given the chance. Then as the time goes along, wow, the alignment that comes from giving them small tasks or opportunities that comport with what they shared with you builds their confidence that what they say really matters."

He told us about a member of his team who was the hub of coordination in the office. "But," he said, "she was starting to feel like a reporting mechanism and wasn't being given a chance to think creatively or strategically. She had this skill set as a conductor that was highly regarded, but it felt limiting to her." While some managers might encourage the employee to lean into this strength, Helfrich knew that if she wasn't allowed to stretch and grow, he might lose her. He asked if the employee would like to take the lead on a new project, allowing her to guide the creative process, which, he says, "unlocked career growth that wouldn't have happened otherwise."

To conduct such development conversations, we recommend asking the following questions:

- What activities do you look forward to doing most at work?
- What is it about those tasks that energizes you?
- What tasks frustrate you?
- What is it about those tasks that's demotivating?
- If you had a few wishes for your career, what would they be?
- Is there anything else you're curious about that you haven't been able to explore yet in your career?

In order to capture what you learn from this and subsequent, ongoing conversations, we advise taking the approach recommended by Dr. Sydney Finkelstein, professor of management at Dartmouth College. He suggests managers create spreadsheets into which they enter the following information for each employee:

+ General observations about working style and an assessment of the person's potential.

+ Feedback received about ways the person likes to be managed.

+ Key motivators, including extrinsic rewards like financial compensation or manager-to-employee recognition as well as intrinsic drivers such as excelling in their work or having ownership of their decisions and actions.

+ Possible opportunities for career enhancement, including what networking, stretch assignments, and promotion targets might be needed.

+ The person's stated long-term career and development goals.

+ Feedback the leader needs to offer to help the person grow (including broader wisdom about the industry the leader wishes to impart over time).

Then, before each development conversation, a quick perusal of their information can help pinpoint issues to follow up on that might have gone by the wayside in the hustle of day-to-day operations. Perhaps an employee said he'd like to present the team with an idea for improving a process, and you'd forgotten about that over the past few weeks. A ten-minute review of the spreadsheet allows you to put it back on the table and propose a first step for him to take.

Method 7: Carefully Calibrate Growth Opportunities

Employees who want to stretch their wings may not always be ready to fly. People differ dramatically in how well they assess their preparedness for new challenges; some who are anxious may shy away when they are more than ready, while others champing at the bit need a good deal of growth yet. For an inexperienced employee, a small role on a cross-functional team might be an ideal opportunity to see more tenured teammates in action and learn how other areas of the company operate. For a more seasoned worker, a leadership opportunity on a project may be appropriate.

Margaret Rogers, vice president of Pariveda Solutions, a technology consulting firm, shared an example of a manager who has two employees who have an interest in developing their public speaking skills. "From previous meetings, you know one of them is less experienced and more nervous about talking in public," she said. "This employee might benefit more from a small group setting, like a lunch-and-learn, during which he gives a short presentation. Because the other employee has had more practice, you might have her fly solo and present on a topic at the next companywide meeting or at a conference in front of a larger audience."

Rogers also recommends varying the level of control employees have over their own development based on their experience. A more seasoned employee should be given greater latitude to select opportunities for growth, while more guidance will be required for a new hire. But even with recruits, such as those fresh out of college, it's crucial to allow some degree of input into the process. It's also important to allow for stretching that might lead to some mistakes made, or even a failure on a project, within reasonable constraints, of course. Running into difficulties and experiencing failures can lead to powerful learning experiences and help identify skill gaps, which leaders and employees can then determine ways to fill. The key to reduce anxiety is that people should be coached that setbacks are considered learning opportunities, and a potential failure should never be significantly damaging to the employee's overall performance, or that of the team. For example, asking a new person to make a presentation pitching an improvement idea to the team in a staff meeting might offer a chance to make a persuasive case, but success or failure isn't going to negatively impact results.

With effective coaching, leaders can help an employee who doesn't quite get something right to understand the experience was a terrific demonstration of initiative and creative thinking, rather than a failure. The employee can also build awareness of what success in such an endeavor will require. Margaret Rogers comments in this regard, "Remember, safety is necessary when confidence is low, but pushing employees to the edge of discomfort results in real development."

Method 8: Encourage Peer-to-Peer Support

Today, when an employee wants to learn a new skill, their first stop is rarely their boss. Most younger workers will go online—to Google or YouTube—or will consult with their friends inside or outside the organization through crowdsourcing. It can be anxiety-inducing to wait for a manager to make time for you, and sometimes it creates anxiety to admit you don't know something. Effective leaders embrace peer-to-peer learning.

Dr. LaMesha Craft of National Intelligence University says peer learning can be "the most powerful tool in the workplace." People are more likely to more candidly ask about things they don't understand or are having trouble with when talking with peers. Also, so much of the expertise that makes businesses run well isn't in the heads of leaders, or in a training manual or formal process, it's learned from hands-on experience and kept in the collective know-how of employees. Team members can share a wealth of "learning by doing" knowledge with one another, and they are building a culture of continuous learning along the way.

Organizations are encouraging peers to assist one another with their day-to-day work, and with networking and pursuing learning opportunities, in a myriad of creative ways. Many firms we work with have set up online marketplaces on their intranets to facilitate this, while others hold peer-learning workshops to connect employees who are willing to teach specific skills to their colleagues.

Another great practice that can be less anxiety-producing for introverted employees than giving a presentation is asking them to create how-to videos on important processes, which are posted on the company's internal network. Some might also be shown to new employees when they come on board. Generally, three to four minutes is the optimal length, and a wealth of free filmmaking services are available online, along with tutorials about best practices for recording and editing.

In their book *The Expertise Economy*, Kelly Palmer and

David Blake advocate formalizing peer-to-peer learning to build employee confidence. They point to a few characteristics that summarize best practices that can get a team learning more from each other and peers around the organization:

1. **Appoint a facilitator.** Assign a person who can organize peer-learning sessions and keep meetings on topic, whether in person or online.

2. **Build a safe environment.** Help participants feel safe to ask questions and share thoughts and experiences. Invite specialists to "parachute" in from other departments and pick their brains.

3. **Focus on real-world situations.** Team members are more likely to participate, and learn more effectively, if learning sessions address their current challenges.

*   *   *

While there are many uncertainties today, especially about the working world, we are certain that those leaders who will be successful in the future will give greater attention to people development. To solve the seemingly intractable problems of our time, and to move our organizations in a more prosperous direction, great bosses will pay more attention to their people—especially finding ways for them to grow. Success going forward will depend largely on finding ways to bring the unique motivators, style, and talents of our people to bear.

Help Chart Career Development

- Research shows younger workers are more eager to move up or out, and more than 75 percent of Gen Zers say they believe they should be promoted within their first year on the job. Creating more steps on the career path can help.

- Some 90 percent of younger workers "highly value" career growth and development opportunities, and organizations that effectively nurture their people's desire to learn are 30 percent more likely to be market leaders.

- Some 87 percent of millennials ranked job security as a top priority when looking for a job. That is more than likely going to be even higher in the post-pandemic world.

- Following a set of methods can reduce employees' anxiety about where they're heading in their careers. They include: 1) create more steps to grow, 2) coach employees about how to get ahead, 3) help employees assess their skills and motivations, 4) use a skill development flow, 5) make learning real-time, 6) tailor development to the individual, 7) carefully calibrate growth opportunities, and 8) encourage peer-to-peer support.

SUMMARY

How "It's Not Perfect" Can Become "It's Good, I'll Move On"

HELP TEAM MEMBERS MANAGE PERFECTIONISM

—

A beautiful thing is never perfect.

—Egyptian proverb

While the term "perfectionism" implies an extreme pursuit of the flawless—and is generally understood as an affliction—our culture has fostered it in many ways. Schools have become breeding grounds for perfectionism, offices as well. Perfectionism is too often mistaken for admirable stick-to-it-iveness, having excellence in standards, and a healthy ambition. In fact, once upon a time, we were told "I'm a perfectionist" was the recommended answer to the hackneyed interview question: "What's your biggest flaw?"—mocked by cultural satirists *The Simpsons*. When asked in a job interview at the Springfield Nuclear Power Plant for their worst quality, those applying answered:

Applicant 1: *Well, I am a workaholic.*
Applicant 2: *Well, I push myself too hard.*

Only clueless Homer Simpson answered honestly.

Homer: *Well, it takes me a long time to learn anything. I'm kind of a goof-off. Little stuff starts disappearing from the workplace.*

Why shouldn't we strive for perfection in our work? The fact is, some people should. We rightfully want a technician processing our blood sample to do everything by the book. Airline pilots have little to no room for error, which is why they have copilots and plenty of electronic help. In lots of professions, and with certain aspects of each job, flawless execution is vital. We have worked for many years with groups at Intel, for instance, and there are few companies that value perfection more in their manufacturing process. As with many industrial organizations, Intel seeks zero variations once a process is optimized.

Thus, there are times when people are absolutely right to hold themselves to extremely exacting standards. They're not being perfectionists in these times, they're being responsible. Perfectionism isn't about a rational quest to get things right when they have to be, it's a corrosive impulse to appear perfect, and often to push others to perfection as well (while being averse to any criticism themselves). And, in a horrible irony, perfectionism can seriously undermine people's performance and has become a warning sign for many employers.

Consider the case of one of the greatest performers of all time, opera star Maria Callas.

In the 1940s and '50s, Callas became one of classical music's bestselling vocalists, and today is still considered by many to be the greatest soprano of all time. She forever changed expectations of singers with an acting talent that had never been seen on the opera stage. And yet Callas's career is an example of how striving for perfection can eat away at excellence.

Pushed by an overbearing mother—who had her singing on the street for money as early as age five—as the *Washington Post* reported, she developed a "perfectionism that grew ever more fierce as her voice decayed." Callas pushed herself to be flawless at the expense of her health and relationships at work and outside. On one occasion, before a rehearsal at La Scala, she was asked to wait until the eminent pianist Wilhelm Backhaus finished rehearsing a concerto in the space Callas was scheduled for. Callas refused adamantly, saying she didn't care who it was: "I'm supposed to start my rehearsal at three o'clock. Tell him it's over." While rehearsing *Medea*, she rushed to a nearby café during a break from a rehearsal, where she was asked, "What are you holding?" She was still grasping the prop dagger, her mind unable to take a break from her role.

While a one-in-a-lifetime talent, Callas's expectations of

perfection weighed so heavily that she eventually had a hard time performing. In recapping her career, she said, "I never lost my voice, but . . . I lost my courage." Her singing days were over by age forty, where in contrast, Joan Sutherland, considered to be history's second-best soprano after Callas, was able to sing into her midsixties.

While aiming for excellence can lead to breakthroughs, perfectionism can lead to breakdowns.

The Endless Report Card

Perfectionists aren't merely ambitious, diligent strivers. As Dr. Brian Swider of the University of Florida, who's researched the differences between strivers and perfectionists, says, "Yes, perfectionists strive to produce flawless work, and have higher levels of motivation and conscientiousness than nonperfectionists. However, they are also more likely to set inflexible and excessively high standards, to evaluate their behavior overly critically, to hold an all-or-nothing mindset about their performance ('my work is either faultless or a total failure'), and to believe their self-worth is contingent on performing perfectly. Studies have also found that perfectionists have higher levels of stress, burnout, and anxiety."

For those who struggle with perfectionism, life is an endless report card about their accomplishments, looks, quality of friends, and so on. And that is a fast track to unhappiness and a great deal of worry. A key difference between unhealthy perfectionism and healthy striving is being able to define realistic expectations and knowing when to say "that's good enough."

A particularly subversive aspect of perfectionism, which perfectionists themselves generally aren't aware of, is that they're not actually driven so much to *be* perfect as much as to be *seen* as perfect, which leads them to be obsessed with not failing, holding themselves to unattainable standards, and avoiding public mistakes at all costs. As such, they can spend so much time tinkering or deciding on a course of action that they get little done.

In addition, perfectionists often feel a heightened need for positive validation and approval, while dreading any form of negative judgment or criticism. Research shows that perfectionism can lead people to put in less effort, not more—with their subconscious leading them to reason: "Since I'm not going to get this exactly right, I won't try as hard." And the vicious effect is this creates more pressure when people fall behind and feel criticized for inadequate work.

Benjamin Cherkasky, a therapist and researcher on perfectionism at Northwestern University's Family Institute, understands that twisted logic firsthand. He says he quit a competitive swim team when he was in the eighth grade even though he loved the sport. The thing was, he wasn't winning as many races as he thought he should. "I'm not Michael Phelps, so why am I even on the team?" Cherkasky recalls thinking. He realized only years later that unrealistic standards were taking the joy out of his time in the pool.

One final effect of perfectionism is that it may cause people to isolate themselves and detach from their work and from others. It can cause overwhelming emotional suffering and act as both a cause and symptom of anxiety.

While perfectionism has long been a problem among employees, in recent years, it's become a good deal more common. In a 2017 study led by Thomas Curran of the University of Bath in England, the team analyzed data from more than forty thousand American, Canadian, and British college students, showing that the majority had significantly higher scores than previous generations on measures of: irrational personal desire to never fail; perceiving excessive expectations from others; and placing unrealistic standards on those around them.

There is plenty of research to suggest that social media is contributing to this rising fear of failure, pressuring young adults to compare their own work achievements to their peers' (usually unfavorably), as is worry about achieving high marks for those in school. The motivation of many college students who strive to produce only perfect results is driven by fears of negative outcomes. The paradigm shift from "Cs get degrees" to "I'll never be able to afford a mortgage if I don't get into a good grad program" has provided many students a somber motivation to strive for flawlessness and ramped up levels of worry, stress, and anxiety. If there's one thing the college admission scandal of 2019 taught us, it's that the anxiety students and parents feel is palpable and can push those with wealth and power to make terrible decisions. The message for youth was unfortunate: Successful people should do whatever they can to get ahead, even if it means cheating.

Back in our day (the early fourteenth century), most studious high school students just hoped to get into university—any university, really. But in the modern world, students are driven to achieve near-perfect GPAs to get into the "right" school, and then to keep excelling to get into prestigious graduate schools. To accomplish this, rich families hire tutors and send their kids on elaborate community service trips to boost their resumes, while students from economically disadvantaged families usually have to work part-time or full-time to pay for tuition, leaving less time for study. Universities unwittingly encourage competition by pitting students against each other. Online systems—now used by almost every university—instantly show students their scores on each assignment and test compared with the mean and class highs.

Anthony admits checking his university's online Canvas system at least once an hour on days his test scores would post. It took him until his senior year to realize the wisdom of just putting his head down and working hard to learn, grades be damned. "Early in my college years I'd grown frustrated when I realized I wasn't going to be able to master every concept when taking four or five science classes at once. If I wanted to be able to grasp the next concept, sometimes I had to move on with just a basic understanding of some ideas."

Anthony said his freshman year he had been so stressed that he withdrew from a class because he had started the semester with a C average in that class and then got a D on his midterm. "I probably could have pulled through and gotten a passing grade had I just adopted the mindset that I was there to learn, was new at this science stuff, and even a C would be good enough in my first hard science class."

He had been driven by a system that rewards high grades over becoming well-educated. In such places, grading drives uniformity. There is no place for risk, adventure, or genuine learning when your only goal is to please a professor and get an A. Students start to treat the entire thing as a game, working just hard enough to survive so they can move to the next level. Near the end of his life, Albert Einstein told the New York State Education Department, "A society's competitive advantage will come not from how well its schools teach the multiplication and periodic tables, but how well they stimulate imagination and creativity."

How to Spot It

Before addressing what a manager can do to help perfectionist employees stay on track and meet their deadlines, it's important to briefly share some insights about different types of perfectionism and how to spot them in a team.

The work of Paul Hewitt of the University of British Columbia and Gordon Flett of York University in Toronto has clarified that there are three basic types of perfectionism. When focused inward, toward the *self*, perfectionism leads individuals to hold unrealistic expectations of themselves and make punitive self-evaluations. This is self-oriented perfectionism. Alternatively, when people perceive demands for perfection coming *from others*—bosses, spouses, friends, even strangers—leading them to believe they must be perfect to gain approval from the world—they're suffering from socially prescribed perfectionism. Finally, when perfectionistic expectations are directed *toward others*, people impose unrealistic standards on those around them. This is other-oriented perfectionism.

These are by no means mutually exclusive; people might be under the sway of several or all of them. But knowing about the differences is helpful in considering the best means of assisting employees. We can ask ourselves, Is an employee beating himself up, making critical comments about himself or his work? Does one worker seem to be thinking you're expecting more of her than you are? Is another employee overly critical of the work done by colleagues or subordinates?

In terms of spotting that someone is a perfectionist, Dr. Alice Boyes, former clinical psychologist and author of *The Anxiety Toolkit*, advises that they might seek excessive guidance, seem loath to take any sort of risk, and treat every decision as if it were a matter of life and death. It's a good assumption to make that those displaying perfectionist tendencies have anxiety.

Harvard University research adds that perfectionists tend to become overly defensive when criticized. Healthy strivers, by contrast, tend to take criticism in stride as they push for superior results. And while strivers tend to bounce back from failures, perfectionists often become preoccupied with their missteps or the mistakes of others.

Okay, so what's to be done to help these employees? What follows are a series of methods we've found are helping in leading those with perfectionist tendencies.

Method 1: Clarify What Good Enough Is

First, take a little time to consider whether you, or the organizational culture, might be stoking perfectionism in those with a tendency toward it. In our coaching of leaders, we often find that they push themselves and their team members to not only high standards, but unrealistic ones. In this way, leaders can become overly harsh in criticizing employee work, and their focus on addressing problems and putting fires out takes up so much of their time that it leads many to overlook offering praise to their people—ramping up anxiety considerably. Well-calibrated and well-timed recognition of good work can help everyone feel more confident that they're doing all they can to help the team. It can also help people learn the boundaries of what counts as acceptable work—when good enough is good enough.

If left entirely on their own to determine whether their work is up to snuff, perfectionists are more than likely to overthink and rework, make tweaks, second-guess, or even do too much—such as doing inventory for everyone instead of only on the products they were asked to count, or handing in *War and Peace* when their boss really wanted an executive summary. We know that most managers have no desire to handhold their people, and they rightfully worry about micromanaging, but with employees who tend toward perfectionism it's important to guide them clearly through the standards you're looking for.

Anthony recounts how helpful this was when he transitioned from working in chemistry labs to biotechnology labs. "In chem labs, we were accurate in weighing and measuring re-agents to several decimal places," he said. "It was time-consuming and several hours were allotted to make measurements accurate. The scales were surrounded by windshields to keep our breath off, and the reading on the scale could change if we leaned against the counter. When I got into my first biotech lab, I sought that same level of accuracy."

As he delicately used a scoop to measure out a portion of agar (seaweed jelly)—lifting tiny amounts back and forth between the scale and the container—his lab leader stepped in. She explained that such perfectionism was not necessary in this biotechnology procedure. They were making jelly for bacteria to eat, not splitting the atom. "She helped me break the habit," he says, "which allowed me to devote more time to the things that did need more accuracy. It definitely made me a more proficient lab worker."

Dr. Boyes recommends being clear with employees that they can deem some work less important than other tasks, and setting guidelines for them to follow, which she has seen can greatly reduce anxiety in perfectionists. She also advises assigning mentors to walk junior employees through their work, showing them how they get things done and sharing examples of what is a good standard.

Method 2: Share the Wisdom of Innovators

There's been a great deal written in recent years about the wisdom of starting with a "minimum viable product" when it comes to creating innovations. Minimum viable, note, does not mean crappy. It means a solid product that is ready for testing with consumers so that you can then make improvements to make the product great, if not eventually perfect. That process, known as the lean startup approach, has been greatly helping companies speed up product and services development and deliver final products that are better because customers have input into the design.

Columbia Business School professor Rita McGrath told us a learning-on-the-go approach is helpful in alleviating people's fear of failure—a big issue for perfectionists. If employees are worried about "a failure blotting their record," she said, "it's easier not to make a decision or to make a diffused decision." This can be serious business. According to new research from Forrester Consulting, one-third of all products are delivered late or incomplete due to an inability or delay in decision-making.

McGrath has a great way of addressing concerns about failure on creating an on-the-go learning culture, a recommendation managers should discuss with all their staff members and not just their perfectionists. She highlights, "In an innovative organization, you want to encourage individuals to take initiative." Each person's input to the process can evolve, but if they don't go ahead and put their idea or work product out there for evaluation, then whatever "mutations" might make it better can't be discovered. When it comes to innovation, she says, "It's true that most mutations don't work out, but the ones that break through do so in a big way." The same is fundamentally true with employees learning to achieve the excellence perfectionists so strive for. We advise that managers coach their people that it's better to get their work done on time, as well as they can, and put something out there for evaluation. This way, they can get input from other team members, leaders, even customers, and not be locked in a mental prison of anxious worry.

Constantly moving forward like this is a great way of helping perfectionists, and all staff, cultivate a "growth mindset."

Stanford psychologist Carol Dweck introduced that term in her bestselling book *Mindset*, which we recommend to all managers. Her research revealed that people tend to have either a growth mindset, meaning they believe their intelligence and aptitude can be developed and are willing to try new strategies and seek help from others; or they have a fixed mindset, which leads them to believe that their intelligence is carved in stone, and their aptitudes for certain kinds of work won't develop much over time, e.g., "I'm just not good with technology." This causes them to shy away from new challenges. In addition, people with a growth mindset tend to perceive criticism about their work as constructive and as helping them improve. Developing a growth mindset helps people dive into whatever work they might find daunting and not suffer from anxiety about getting it done, or from self-punishment if they've got to make improvements.

We talked with one senior executive who admitted he has perfectionist tendencies. He has benefited greatly from his own boss coaching him to view the work he and his team were doing through a growth-mindset perspective. Darcy Verhun, the president of FYidoctors, told us, "I tend to push myself and I am aware that can lead to a tendency for me to push others too hard."

He shared an example with us: "A few years ago we created a visual interpretation of our goals using a series of increasingly higher mountains. We had our goals bannered at the top of each mountain. We called it 'Expedition.' As we reached a goal, we would put a flag at the top of the mountain we had collectively 'climbed.' When we got to the end of the third quarter, I realized that I couldn't put flags on all the mountains. I hate to fail, so I was sweating as I met with our founder and chairman. We only had hit about 60 percent of our stretch goals. And two of the milestones were complete fails."

Verhun shared with his boss how dismayed he was with the team's performance and his own failure as a leader. The conversation went as follows:

Chairman: *Did you think we were going to achieve all those goals?*
Verhun: *Of course, we put them on paper and the team all agreed to them.*

Chairman: *Darcy, if we had achieved all our goals, that would have been an indication that we weren't dreaming big enough.*
Verhun: *But two of the milestones were epic fails. They'll never be achieved.*
Chairman: *Did you learn something from them?*
Verhun: *Yeah, a ton.*
Chairman: *Okay, great. And I'm guessing we will apply the lessons we learned from any mistakes we made along the way?*
Verhun: *Yes.*
Chairman: *Awesome. Carry on. See you next quarter.*

Verhun says he's told this story on many occasions at every level in his company. "It is such a great example of our ethos: We are going to try things, fine-tune as we learn, fix mistakes, and produce results together. We will never be perfect, but we will always strive for excellence," he said. We think the wisdom this chairman imparted is a great story to share with all perfectionists.

Ryan Westwood, cofounder and CEO of Simplus, told us, "It helps tremendously with perfectionism when leaders are open about their own anxieties. It puts people at ease and gives everyone permission to be human. We did a leadership training last week, and I told a story about how I screwed up in the way we structured management incentives in our latest acquisition. We failed to maximize the benefits of the team. I talked about how hard it was to navigate through it and how much it stressed me. It was almost like there was this collective sigh of relief by employees on the call. They were posting on the thread about how it was so nice to hear their CEO had messed up."

Another manager we interviewed about this issue shared a great message he reinforces in his firm. Roland Ligtenberg is the founder of Housecall Pro, an eight-year-old San Diego software company with about 150 employees. He has seen firsthand the effects of perfectionism on rising anxiety levels in his firm, so he began coaching his employees: "In our world, perfection is the enemy of *done*."

Of course, even such wise coaching won't be enough to help perfectionists, or most employees, get over their fear of failure if the culture of a team is one that's harsh about making mistakes. So, it's important to openly address with teams that they should readily alert you or their boss about problems, and then you work to solve them together.

Method 3: Treat Failures as Learning Opportunities

During the 2020 pandemic, we were able to listen in on a call with the leadership team of one of our clients—a restaurant chain—the Monday morning after Mother's Day. It was a time when every restaurant needed every dollar to keep the lights on, but the online ordering system had gone down for several hours over the weekend, costing untold thousands of dollars in revenue and upsetting a lot of guests whose orders were never received.

The chief information officer could have been on the hot seat as the call started with leaders around the country whose stores had been affected. Instead, the chief executive leading the session told the group that blame had no place in their culture. "I know we had a tough day yesterday, but we don't point fingers," he said. "No one wanted this to happen, and I appreciate Amir [the CIO] and our IT team responding on a tough day to get us back up and running. Let's have a productive discussion about how we go forward to learn and get better."

What followed was an hour spent brainstorming about potential investments in time, talent, and technology that could help them learn from the setback. By the time Father's Day arrived, the CIO's team had redundant systems in place and a series of backups if anything happened.

This was one of the most constructive examples we've witnessed of a leader assuming positive intent and getting a team working together with the understanding that when failure happens, we can get better as a result.

We have witnessed meetings, in other organizations, that degraded into blame sessions. We've also met with loads of employees who've recounted the damaging effects of being publicly censured for a mistake. Being told off for any employee is like a figurative punch to the brain and can trigger feelings of shame and despondency.

When Alan Mulally assumed the CEO mantle at Ford Motor Company in 2006, he inherited a culture in which an unhealthy fear of failure had infected the leadership ranks. Executive meetings had become places of combat in which employees tried to identify flaws in each other's plans instead of recommending solutions.

Mulally told us he instituted a new philosophy, "based on the fact that we are going to have problems, and we're going to need everybody's help to solve them."

It took weeks to finally convince the leaders they were safe, but in one meeting North American President Mark Fields took a chance and admitted a new vehicle launch under his purview would be delayed. Other executives looked on nervously. Mulally said, "I could see it in people's eyes that they thought doors would open up behind Mark and two large human beings would remove him. 'Bye-bye Mark.'"

Instead, Mulally began a round of applause and said, "Mark, thank you so much. That is great visibility." Then he asked the group, "Is there anything we can do to help Mark out?" Within seconds, ideas were flying around the room.

Said Mulally, the moment passed in the blink of an eye but changed everything. As he frequently told his leaders, "You *have* a problem; *you* are not the problem."

Method 4: Regularly Check In on Progress
While micromanaging is definitely to be avoided, we advise managers that they must keep good track of the progress their team members are making, and this is especially important for perfectionists. Leaders can help them understand that their work is going just fine and uncover procrastination or wrong turns, if that's the case.

A great example of creating a system for checking on progress is that of managers at SpaceX, who found a way to make faster decisions for their biggest client—NASA. Until recently,

NASA sent a fax (seriously) whenever they had a query, and once a week SpaceX brought together a fifty-person team to address each question before sending responses back. Using collaborative technology, SpaceX has now given NASA direct visibility into each project so they can identify the SpaceX engineers who are working on which components. NASA can directly talk with those engineers and make decisions in real time. This collaboration has allowed SpaceX to cut its average wait time for defining product requirements by 50 percent and eliminate the costly weekly four-hour status meeting.

The key in making check-ins less anxiety-inducing is to put more control of these conversations in the hands of employees. Ambiguity creates anxiety, so instead of subjective measures, use individual and team roadmaps to evaluate how people are coming on hitting their goals. Also, make check-ins regular. When they become an expected part of work life, versus surprise inspections, anxiety about reporting in is reduced substantially. Finally, when managers go out of their way to offer up support with problems or missed deadlines during check-ins—and they come from a place of understanding—it can help create a relationship where people know they will be held accountable, but in positive ways. And their manager is there to help them succeed.

Method 5: Team Them Up

Another method for helping perfectionists recognize their tendencies and work to change is to pair them up with employees who don't have the problem.

We heard a terrific example of this from a manager we spoke with. Liz told us one of her sales reps, Sara, was driving her mad with an attention to detail that was not necessary. For example, when it came to her monthly sales reports, Sara's were far more elaborate than Liz needed—including pages of graphs and charts of her sales mix. Liz sat Sara down on several occasions to explain that kind of detail wasn't necessary and was more than any manager could process. Liz wanted her charge to spend her extra time doing more prospecting calls; Sara's cold calls were below average for the team. The months went by, however, and Sara kept turning in reports that way. When challenged, she would say, "I don't mind. It helps me to look at things in this way." In truth, Sara couldn't help herself.

Having realized she would need to take a different approach, Liz applied a strategy that proved more effective. When she found Sara bogged down on unnecessary activities in her work, she paired her with less detail-oriented partners so she would be forced to accept "good enough" results to get the task done by deadline. And, as she began to be praised for her team-oriented, on-time work, Sara began to slowly change. Liz also continued to meet with Sara regularly to help her with her self-awareness. Instead of challenging her to change, Liz invited Sara to be actively involved in her coaching and think of ways that she could improve her sense of urgency on projects and where to devote the bulk of her time.

With patience, said Liz, the result has been a salesperson

who now has increased confidence and self-awareness, and is getting a lot more done.

Method 6: Discuss the Issue Openly
Talking with people about such personal issues as being a perfectionist can be quite uncomfortable, we know. But with the right approach, an honest discussion can really open people's eyes to the issue, and then, with that recognition, make headway. Many people who suffer from perfectionism don't see that's the case. Benjamin Cherkasky is a great example. It took him years, and a graduate degree in counseling psychology from Northwestern, to help him spot his tendencies. The best way we've found to help employees see the problem, and for managers to talk with them about it, is to kindly acknowledge that they clearly like to get things right and that's appreciated. Since discussing the problem that someone seems to be somewhat perfectionistic can lead them to be defensive, the phrasing is important.

Consider this typical well-intended but potentially inflammatory conversation between manager and employee:

Jared, you've got high standards, just like me. I see that you always try to make sure all the details are attended to and everything is done exactly right. That can be a good thing. Now, as I want you to progress in this organization, let me coach you a little. I've had to learn that focusing on improving things from 95 percent to 100 often bogs you down. You can get tunnel vision in getting something perfect that can cost you more than it does to move on to the next project. Let me give you an example of where I saw this with you recently . . .

That's not a terrible conversation. But notice a few subtle differences in the next exchange (in bold), and how the manager personalizes the conversation and deflects blame off Jared to the issue itself.

*Jared, you've got high standards, just like me. I see that you always try to make sure all the details are attended to and everything is done exactly right. That can be a good thing. Now, as I want you to progress in this organization, **I'll tell you something I had to learn.** Focusing on improving things from 95 percent to 100 often **bogs down opportunities. It's easy to get tunnel vision** in getting something perfect that **can cost more than it does to move on to the next project. Let me give you an example I saw where you might have applied this lesson.***

In both examples, the manager relates to Jared right away, expressing common ground with the issue. She lets him know she understands where he is coming from and explains that they both have high standards. Great. This establishes a sense of comfort and connection. And yet in the first example the phrase "let me coach you" we believe would introduce an elephant into the room, letting Jared know that correction was coming and he might need to protect his feelings. In the second exchange, when the manager says, "I'll tell you something I had to learn," it delivers a sense that she's about to offer wisdom gained in the trenches, and the discussion is an opportunity to learn rather than correct. We can just imagine Jared leaning in.

Similarly, in the second example, the manager avoids "you" statements, and refers to the problem with such proclamations as "It's easy to get tunnel vision" instead of "*You* can get tunnel vision." This isn't just a trick of semantics, but an important part of helping team members understand that this is a constructive discussion about a change in behavior that will help the employee learn and grow versus an indictment of their overall worth.

Another good way in these discussions to help perfectionists accept needed improvements to their work, without putting them on the defensive, is asking them to propose solutions—asking what they would do differently in the future to keep their projects on task or make faster decisions.

Now, even with these methods, perfectionists may get their hackles up when receiving feedback, and they might deflect what they see as blame onto others on the team or even their manager (you). This is not acceptable, of course, but it's important to keep in mind that it's a knee-jerk impulse. People who get defensive may have had negative experiences in their past that make them wary of being seen as inadequate. For us, as leaders, signaling that we care about employees' feelings can make them feel more secure and tone down the rhetoric, which can help them be less likely to criticize in the future.

In Chapter 6, we introduce a methodology that can help deliver feedback more directly: Issue, Value, Solution. Instead of saying something such as "You are too negative," you might talk about an issue you have witnessed, e.g., "I want to speak with you about your call with ABC Corp on Thursday." You then relate this to a core value you are trying to live in the team: "One of our values is creating a positive environment for each other and our clients, and as such we attempt to be friendly on every call." And finally, together, you come up with a solution to move forward. If this approach still solicits a defensive response, then a manager should cut the discussion short and move it to another day. A simple "Why don't you think about it and we'll meet again next week to discuss" may allow their defensiveness to tone down and your feedback to sink in.

Manage Perfectionism

- There are certain jobs when flawless execution is vital. Perfectionism isn't about a rational quest to get things right when they have to be; it's a corrosive impulse to appear perfect, and often to push others for flawlessness as well.

- Studies have found perfectionists have higher levels of stress, burnout, and anxiety. They can also spend so much time tinkering or deciding on a course of action that they get little done.

- A key difference between unhealthy perfectionism and healthy striving is being able to define realistic expectations and knowing when to say "that's good enough."

- To identify someone who might have perfectionist tendencies, look for those who seek excessive guidance, seem loath to take any sort of risk, and treat most decisions as if they were a matter of life and death. Perfectionists can also tend to become overly defensive when criticized, and they can become preoccupied with their missteps or the mistakes of others.

- A series of methods can help lead those with perfectionist tendencies, including: 1) clarify what good enough is, 2) share the wisdom of innovators, 3) treat failures as learning opportunities, 4) regularly check in on progress, 5) team them up, and 6) discuss the issue openly.

From Conflict Avoidance to Healthy Debate

HELP TEAM MEMBERS FIND THEIR VOICE

Don't raise your voice, improve your argument.

—Desmond Tutu

A common complaint we hear from managers is that many of their people today are conflict-avoidant—they shy away from disagreements, can't handle honest feedback, and will not engage in tough conversations. This isn't just a handful of wallflowers they are talking about. Some of the highest performing employees we've interviewed admit they sidestep uncomfortable situations and hold back giving honest feedback.

Usually they are worried about keeping their jobs.

Conflict in the workplace can be a significant cause of anxiety for many workers, especially for younger people, and yet debate is inevitable and necessary in the workplace. With that said, we do accept that unhealthy quarreling can spring up among coworkers that can subvert effective teamwork. Managers should address mean-spirited tensions head-on, and team members who stir up hostility should be coached. But there is a big difference between hostility and debate.

Senior leadership advisor Connie Dieken, a multiple Emmy-winning broadcast journalist and author of *Become the Real Deal*, says the level of trust and transparency a leader creates makes a big difference. "It's critical that leaders get this right. A low level of candor in a team can lead to poor performance through defensiveness, hurt feelings, and withholding. When leaders model and invite thoughtful candor, people respond by sharing their ideas and questions directly and honestly, without fear of repercussions or judgment."

In our consulting work, we have been surprised by how much disagreement and strenuous debate we find in high-performance work groups. In these teams of high trust and high candor, the members tell us debates are welcome, drive inventive problem-solving, and can be highly motivating. After all, don't we debate things in every other area of our lives? We find that when team members are free to speak up and know their voices will be heard, it can increase engagement, enhance psychological safety, and over time bolster self-confidence and a sense of ownership. A vigorous exchange of competing perspectives has been shown to improve team performance on numerous fronts, especially in enhancing the development of exciting new ideas.

The best leaders facilitate this by:

- Encouraging a good degree of healthy discussion in a safe environment.

- Setting ground rules for debate and encouraging all voices to be heard.

- De-escalating quarreling with a calming process that brings order and safety to participants.

- Asking team members to clarify their opinions with facts when working through tough issues.

- Creating clear plans and timelines for moving forward after debates conclude.

For employees who are highly conflict-averse, however, when they see debate brewing it can be upsetting and cause them to flee or freeze. Dieken adds that some people will try to sugarcoat things to avoid any conflict: "They'd rather perjure themselves than have an uncomfortable discussion. These are often people-pleasers, perfectionists, the highly anxious. They sidestep so they don't have to deliver unwelcome news, or they hold back for fear that people won't like them or will blame them." Others who have these tendencies retreat into passive-aggressive behaviors. Fearing to speak the truth in a group setting, they are more than happy to keep their opinions to themselves.

To those who are conflict-averse, a handful of team members sharing their views aggressively, or with a great deal of assurance, can feel threatening. To help smooth over tensions among their colleagues, they may intensify their own anxiety by taking undo responsibility in an attempt to quash the debate. Because they so value harmony and relationships, they are usually willing to sacrifice much, including their own mental comfort, to ensure relationships stay intact.

It's possible some use this approach in their personal lives. Some friends may like them because they seem so kind, while others take advantage of the way they avoid conflict. *I know she's allergic to cats, but Jacqueline will take care of Felix while we are away. She's great.* Since the conflict-averse find it hard to say no and don't want to ruffle feathers, they can often feel misused.

From Conflict to Collaboration

It's worth noting how a manager can spot the difference between someone playing a healthy role as a team builder and an employee plagued by conflict aversion. A few clues to help spot the conflict-averse: if they shy away from difficult conversations, even when such discussions are necessary; if they try to change the topic or flee the scene when things get tense; if they get uncomfortable during debates in staff meetings or brainstorming sessions; or if they resist expressing their feelings or thoughts during meetings—yet might display passive-aggressive tendencies afterward or be upset that their voice was not heard.

When managers perceive that a conflict-avoidance issue may exist, they can do a great deal to address it by working with employees to stand up for themselves. They may also help them take time to consider their own opinions before agreeing to anything that might violate their values, and stick to their guns when challenged.

Dieken suggests leaders help their employees understand that sugarcoating is actually a selfish act, and that "candor is a gift. While you may be trying to spare another person's feelings, sugarcoating is a superficial attempt to seem more appealing. If you filter out bad news, you're dooming others. You help people use better judgment when you arm them with accurate information, even if it's not what they want to hear."

In some cases, we've found the culture of an entire team or organization can be conflict-avoidant, which can be an incredible frustration to those workers who want the group to break out of the status quo. When leading a culture like this, managers play a vital role in steering group discussions to be more inclusive. One leader who has begun to embrace this process is Darcy Verhun, president of FYidoctors. He told us, "We're operating through a different lens now—Zoom meetings—and that means not everybody can or will be able to participate verbally in a conversation. The other day, during an important meeting, I had a powerful sense that we weren't utilizing everybody's full intellectual horsepower. So, as we were wrapping up, I stopped and asked each person on the Zoom call, 'What are you thinking about this topic but haven't said?' It turned out to be a game-changing question. We'd already made a decision, but in ten short minutes what we learned from people's responses to my question resulted in us tweaking our decision, making it better and a lot more thoughtful."

Verhun added, "After the call I received emails from the

team saying that with that question I had demonstrated powerful leadership by intentionally including everyone while also being receptive to their views. It made me stop and realize that our entire leadership team needs to behave in a similar inclusive manner for all important decisions. By ensuring all voices have a chance to be heard, it helps team members deal with any uncertainty they may be feeling about a key decision, and feel they are more part of the solution."

Another manager who has brought an inclusive perspective to various leadership roles throughout his career is Mark Beck, who we met when he was a senior leader of Danaher, a seventy thousand–employee science and technology company. He now owns a group of precision manufacturing companies know as B-Square Precision Group. To encourage healthy debate, Beck says, he might take the side of a person whose view is under assault in a meeting, even if he doesn't necessarily agree with it. This isn't gamesmanship, it's to show that the person is offering up a reasonable way of thinking that should be respected. "The attacker usually steps back a little and softens their tone when a leader does that," he says.

Another way Beck ensures his people will continue to offer their views: "When all arguments have been made, a leader has to make a decision," he said. "You can still do it in a way that doesn't seem like someone's won and someone's lost. A leader might say, 'The arguments on both sides have been fantastic. I can see why it would be reasonable to go either way. But we've got to make a decision. Here's why I think we need to go this way.' Then, the next time, people on the team won't be afraid to make a stand. No one will feel like they've lost; each teammate will know the leader appreciates his or her honest input."

Conflict-Avoidant versus Peacemaker

In all this, we do not wish to denigrate the role of a peace-maker in a team. Peacemaking can be an asset not only in one's own career advancement but for a team as a whole. And a person whose nature is to avoid conflict may, in the proper setting, become just the one to play an important part in mending broken fences in a team.

We admire the thinking of Drs. Emma Seppälä of Yale and Kim Cameron of the University of Michigan, whose research shows that employees who make the most positive impact on team performance foster social connections with others on the team and organization, are highly empathetic, go out of their way to help others, and help create a safe team culture that encourages members to express themselves— even if those conversations are difficult.

What Seppälä and Cameron describe as ideal is part peacemaker, part tough guy/gal when debate is necessary. It's a terrific, balanced definition because playing the role of peacemaker can, if taken too far and motivated by an excessive desire to avoid conflict, lead to a good deal of emotional wear and tear and anxiety, especially from self-criticism. Quite a few people we interviewed who suffer from heightened anx-iety told us they feel guilty about conflicts on their team or with their loved ones at home. It's as if they have failed because they can't create peace and tranquility in the lives of all those around them and solve everyone else's problems.

Another problem that occurs at work: Since they try so hard to get along, they can become dumping grounds for excess work. For instance, they may volunteer to pick up the slack from stressed-out colleagues, and this causes them even more anxiety.

The great irony of many of the efforts of the conflict-avoidant to escape drama is that too often it intensifies anxiety for themselves rather than allaying it. Conflict aversion is often a symptom of an unhealthy preoccupation about what other people think of oneself and the belief, deep down, that you aren't good enough or won't be well liked unless you are seen as super congenial. All the more reason, then, for a leader to make sure every team member is encouraged to speak up, and that every opinion is valued.

On the flip side to this are those overwhelming personalities on a team who can create tension through their force of will. These people seem to thrive on conflict. Big egos can't be ignored (literally), and managers must intervene. They must set boundaries (such as no interrupting the speaker during a meeting), give others equal time, and be willing to cut time hogs off politely but firmly and redirect the conversation. It's also important to hold one-on-ones with dominating personalities, to help them understand why the team needs to hear from everyone during debates, and also to let them vent now and then, to get all their thoughts and ideas out without taking up precious group time.

Millennials and Conflict

Younger workers especially can struggle with personal interaction and conflict resolution. Some younger people we've met admit they prefer to text someone they're having a problem with rather than speak by phone or face-to-face. In-person is too personal for many of the rising generation. One millennial, who, ironically, worked in a smartphone store, told us, "I wish I could disable the phone on my phone."

Another interesting twist of the conflict discussion is that many younger workers can misconstrue firmness or disagreement as a reprimand, even when the other person hasn't raised their voice and is not being bad-tempered. In our interviews, an employee showed us a fascinating text string between him and his forty-something boss to illustrate the point. He had received the message late on a Friday and it read:

Boss: *Got your report.*
Employee: *Is everything okay with it?*
Boss: *Haven't dug in too much yet. Enjoy the weekend . . .*

The young employee assumed something was wrong with his report and said he reread it several times that weekend, and even sent the boss a revised version Sunday night. We must admit this seemed like a pretty innocuous text exchange to us. Anthony had to translate for his Gen X and boomer coauthors.

Anthony explained the young man's response to the first

message: "In texting, a period can mean bad news, and in this case came across as 'end of discussion.' But the biggest problem was he simply didn't say 'thank you' or 'good work getting it in on time.' There was no feedback at all."

As to the boss's second text, it was even worse: "What was that ominous ellipsis all about? What in the world was going to happen after the weekend?" asked Anthony. "Without any nonverbal context to frame the punctuation, an anxious reader can easily interpret ambiguous parts of a message as disapproval."

He continued, "Being reprimanded doesn't necessarily have anything to do with volume. It's feeling, 'You're talking *at* me, and not with me.'"

We encouraged the young employee to have a conversation (in person) with his boss about the texts, and he reported back that his manager had seemed to sincerely appreciate the feedback and said that he had no idea his texts could be interpreted that way. Indeed, if anything he thought he was being encouraging to the young guy for hitting his deadline. The boss promised to update his texting awareness in the future.

Linda Gravett, a Cincinnati-based psychologist, notes that "companies can best help millennials—and all staffers, for that matter—by treating generational issues such as this as a matter of workplace diversity. . . . Age, education, communication style" are dimensions of diversity, and we need to think about them in that way.

Deb Muller, CEO of HR Acuity, notes that many young workers place a high value on harmony and want to work in a place that *feels* good. "Couple a lack of in-person communication with a high desire for harmony and you have an entire group of people who are largely, many believe, extremely conflict-averse." She suggests leaders try to help their team members understand *why* conflict can be a necessary instigator of change for the better. "Any employee who verbally voices concerns or properly navigates conflict situations should be encouraged and applauded."

We've seen managers reward such acts publicly and encourage them as well. For instance, if they aren't getting anyone on the team to step up and challenge the status quo, they'll ask an employee or two to serve as foils during meetings and speak up and argue with the boss, to show that debate is encouraged.

Finally, it's imperative that managers lead by example in this process by being open to new ideas and willing to accept challenges themselves. Yet Dr. David B. Peterson, former head of executive coaching and development for Google, told us, "If you are not genuinely curious and not willing to change your mind, people will figure it out. *Why ask us for our opinions? You are just going to do what you want anyway.*"

He adds, most managers *are* more experienced, have a broader perspective, and are armed with more information, so it's disingenuous if they ask for input they won't use. "When you are in the face of complexity, when you are staring at fog and there are no answers, that's when dialogue and conversation and engagement are really important," he said. Seeking feedback in those times can not only generate real breakthroughs but create an environment where everyone feels valued and engaged.

What follows are a few other methods that managers can use to coach their employees to find their voices and work through issues openly and honestly.

Method 1: Address the Issue, Value, Solution

When discussing any tough subject, a way that may help is by describing the *Issue* succinctly: "Sam, you made a sales call on Landex." That's about it. You state the facts as you know them, and you don't complicate matters. Of course, Sam might go on the defensive if he feels under attack personally, so it's important to associate the issue with your desired team culture. So second, you talk about a team *Value* that is in jeopardy. "Since Landex is in my territory, I can't help but feel that this is not living our value of Working Together." Without that core value of Working Together, Sam's actions might have been completely justified. Third, you brainstorm together on a *Solution*. "Can we come up with a plan to move forward with this account?" It's helpful to proceed in the flow from Issue to Value to Solution. If you jump ahead and start by pointing out that a value has been violated, e.g., "Sam, I'd like to talk to you about our value of Working Together," you can create ambiguity and leave variables for Sam to fill in on his own. He has to guess what you'll say next, and it could be negative. If you come out leading with the facts, the predictive part of the mind that induces anxiety has nothing to work with. Or, if you try to solve a problem without a clear discussion of the issue and how that affects your team values, e.g., "Sam, what are we going to do about Landex?" then you may never learn the real reasons for his actions.

Method 2: Don't Delay

"Although deferring a difficult conversation can result in temporary relief, things simmer, problems get worse, and projects get off track or fail," says Amy Jen Su, managing partner of Paravis Partners, a leadership development firm. When managers display what candor looks like themselves—addressing problems immediately, and with care, empathy, and directness—the message spreads throughout a team that this is appropriate behavior.

In addition, as a leader works with conflict-averse employees, she may have the employee consider what would boost confidence in dealing with the conflict immediately versus putting it off. Does the employee need support during the meeting, or to role-play what might be said? Has the employee considered what business objectives are at risk by not confronting the issue in a timely manner?

Method 3: Stick to Facts

Leaders should teach employees to provide evidence around issues of concern when a conflict ensues. "By naming names, identifying events, describing situations, and illustrating behaviors, the leader seeks to get down to basics," write Drs. Tim Porter-O'Grady and Kathy Malloch, authors of *Quantum Leadership*. A goal of conflict resolution is to ensure that all the tangible issues are laid on the table in clear enough terms that all the players can see them plainly. When the facts are fully presented, it's remarkable how quickly many conflicts can be resolved. With that said, ensure your people have accurate and relevant sources to glean facts from. Also help them understand how you want them to research the issue they will discuss and debate, including what you consider a credible source (e.g., internal reports, industry journals) and what is not (e.g., Wikipedia, social media).

Method 4: Use Your Words

Amy Edmondson of Harvard Business School told us managers must teach their people to have the courage to "use their words" to convey what they see, think, worry about, and need help with. She said, "Many leaders fail to recognize the implications of silence in moments when people could have spoken up. The surprise is how often the use of words is stymied by interpersonal anxiety." That doesn't mean meetings must get bogged down in endless clarification and discussions. Psychologically safe meetings don't have to take longer. What it does mean is managers must show vulnerability and admit they don't have all the answers. Otherwise people are sizing up the situation: "If I get the sense that you don't think you're a fallible human being, like the rest of us, I'm sure as heck not going to stick my neck out." And, she adds, it means leaders must ask essential questions. "Most people will respond to a genuine and direct question. If you ask me what I think, it's mighty awkward *not* to open my mouth."

Method 5: Assume Positive Intent

Team leaders can also teach their people that when debating or facing a tough issue with others in the group, it's important to assume everyone brings positive intentions and wants to do what's right for the organization as a whole—and they are just coming at things from a different perspective. In short, it's okay to question someone's facts or ideas, but not their motives. We'll write about a Republican in Chapter 8, to be fair, but we thought a terrific example of this idea was shared by Democrat Joe Biden in his 2018 eulogy of Republican John McCain. Biden began his talk with these words: "I'm a Democrat, and I loved John McCain. . . . I always thought of John as a brother, [and] we had a hell of a lot of family fights." Biden noted that when he and McCain were junior senators, it was considered appropriate to challenge the opposition's judgment but never to challenge their intentions. That, he said, eventually changed and partisanship emerged as the rule of the day. "All we do today is attack the oppositions of both parties—their motives—not the substance of their argument. The last day John was on the Senate floor he was fighting to restore what you call regular order, to treat one another again like we used to . . . [when we would watch] Teddy Kennedy and James O. Eastland fight like hell on civil rights and then go have lunch together, down in the Senate dining room."

Method 6: Have a Plan

Before their teams set out to tackle a challenge, we recommend leaders coach the conflict-averse to plan and then rehearse what they may say, again with a focus on using the facts they have assembled, e.g., you might help an employee express herself as such: "I've had to pull late nights for a week straight to hit the deadline because you haven't gotten your share of research in on time." Here, presenting the concern clearly, along with facts about the amount of work being done, lays a good base for a conversation about values and a solution rather than the problem itself. Another part of planning is planning to follow up, even if things seem to go well in a first conversation. After all, those involved may have additional thoughts, or they may replay the conversation in their minds and change their point of view, or they may confer with others and come to second-guess the outcome. What we all thought was a positive resolution can begin to deteriorate without follow-up.

Method 7: Give and Take

Leaders must help their employees understand that compromise is inevitable in any debate, and the eventual winner must be the team, not an individual. Say Porter-O'Grady and Malloch, "Each party is looking for something, and unless this something is obtained or willingly given up for something else, the conflict will not end." This means each side has to be able to clearly explain what they want, and each must leave the conflict feeling they obtained something of value and that the other party was given something that was acceptable. This does not mean that what everyone gets will be equal or exactly what they wanted, but it has to be enough to satisfy those involved and the outcome must feel like it's the best for the organization as a whole.

Method 8: Get Comfortable with the Uncomfortable

Of course, despite the best laid plans, any tough conversation can deteriorate into disagreement, hurt feelings, or defensiveness. Managers can help their people prepare for this worst-case by playing out a couple of possible scenarios so that they're ready for whatever may occur. Says Amy Jen Su of Paravis Partners, "When the going gets tough, make sure you don't backpedal, change your message in an attempt to diffuse the situation, or start talking too much to fill silences or plow through the conversation. You want to give the person adequate time to digest what you are saying." So, if the other party starts to get defensive or emotional, leaders should coach the conflict-averse to acknowledge the tension and offer a break instead of demurring. Leaders may also help their team members by giving them language that can help when things get tricky in debates, such as: "Okay, thanks. I understand what you're saying. That helps me know where you are coming from," or "Can you give me more background on your approach so I can understand it better?" In this way, people truly listen with the goal of empathy, not to win but to gain understanding and reach the best outcome for the team.

Bringing It All Together

Using these methods, managers can aid in the process of stirring healthy debate without forcing their team members to change who they are at their core. Part of this is in helping people understand that disagreeing does not necessarily mean two factions are at war, and the process of debate is not to prove who's right and wrong. Debate is part of a healthy work culture, and it's about standing up for what you feel is right while also being open to learning more about others' perspective and intent (which is different from divisive arguments they may have watched on cable news or in heated family gatherings where no one wants to learn anything new, just ram home their point of view). Healthy debates are about ensuring that problems are confronted honestly so we learn from each other and chart the best foreseeable course in the future.

Author Liz Wiseman summed this up beautifully. She learned how to conduct great debates not from her time as a senior executive at Oracle, but from a group of third graders. She had volunteered in her daughter's class to facilitate something called the Junior Great Books Debate. "The third graders would read a story and then the teachers wanted them to argue about it. I thought that would be an easy job, but I got sent off to a day of training to learn how."

Wiseman said she was taught the three rules for debate. Number one: It's a leader's job to ask the question, but never answer it.

Number two: Ask for evidence. For instance, "When one of the children would say Jack climbed the beanstalk because he was greedy, I would say, 'Do you have evidence for that? Can you prove it?' In the first couple of sessions, the kids were terrified. Then they learned they didn't get to have an opinion without something to base it on. So they would turn to page eighteen and point out that Jack stole the white hen and golden harp, so that's why they believed this." (We wish every manager would make note of this idea in facilitating conversations and before making any decision.)

Number three, she said, is to ask everyone. The instructors taught Wiseman to keep a chart with each student listed and put a check mark next to the child's name every time one commented. "I was thinking: I can track that in my head. But I tried this, and it made a big difference. It allowed me to say, 'Robert, we've heard from you twice, but Marcus, we haven't heard from you. We'd like to hear from you before we move on.' It allowed everyone to participate."

Wiseman told us the debate tips immediately made her a better leader.

Manage Healthy Debate

- Many people today are conflict-avoidant—sidestepping uncomfortable situations and holding back on giving honest feedback.

- The best work groups are places of high trust and high candor, where team members debate to drive problem-solving. When employees are free to speak up and know their voices will be heard, it can increase engagement, enhance psychological safety, and bolster self-confidence and a sense of ownership.

- Leaders facilitate this by encouraging debate in a safe environment. They set ground rules and encourage all voices to be heard, de-escalate quarreling, ask team members to clarify their opinions with facts, and create clear plans and timelines for moving forward.

- Managers can spot employees who may be conflict-averse if they shy away from difficult conversations, try to change the topic or flee the scene when things get tense, get uncomfortable during debates, or resist expressing their feelings or thoughts during meetings.

- Methods that managers can use to coach their employees to find their voices and work through difficult conversations include: 1) address the Issue, Value, Solution, 2) don't delay, 3) stick to facts, 4) use your words, 5) assume positive intent, 6) have a plan, 7) give and take, and 8) get comfortable with the uncomfortable.

SUMMARY

Become an Ally

HELP MARGINALIZED TEAM MEMBERS FEEL VALUED AND ACCEPTED

In recognizing the humanity of our fellow beings, we pay ourselves the highest tribute.

—Thurgood Marshall

Many people in leadership roles do not fully understand that bias still occurs in our work cultures, and some unfortunately don't believe it exists at all—dismissing this issue as people being overly sensitive to political correctness. Yet in conducting interviews for this book, it became starkly apparent that there has been a historic pattern of anxiety in particular groups within the workplace—those too often made to feel like "others." Those at the most risk are women, people of color, those on the LGBTQ+ spectrum, members of religious minorities, and those with disabilities (note that this isn't an

exhaustive list). Each of these groups has faced unique oppression in the world at large, and it is mirrored in the workplace with significant implications on their productivity and
engagement and our organizational success.

Understanding, as leaders, how to be allies with all individuals and foster a diverse and inclusive conversation is the
beginning of change.

In writing this chapter, we did not wish to speak over voices
within these communities and the insight they have. What
we'll present here will be eye-opening information about the
real ways that discrimination can lead to significant anxiety
in the workplace for marginalized groups. And we will high-
light the thoughts of those who belong to some of these communities to best help leaders understand better how to help
these individuals thrive.

Not All Anxiety Is Equal

Mental health issues do not care about your race, gender,
or identity; anyone can experience the challenges of anxiety.
But socioeconomic disparities—such as exclusion from
health, educational, social, and economic resources—often
contribute to rates of psychological distress in minority communities. For instance, according to Dr. Thomas Vance of
Columbia University Irving Medical Center, Black people are
20 percent more likely to experience serious mental health
problems than other groups. Yet only 30 percent of Black

adults with mental illness receive treatment annually, com-pared with the US average of 43 percent.

According to Vance, the increased incidence of psycholog-ical difficulties in the Black community is related to a lack of access to proper resources for treatment; prejudice and rac-ism in the daily environment; and issues related to economic insecurity, violence, and criminal injustice.

Equally eye-opening are the mental health challenges of people of lesbian, gay, bisexual, transgender, queer or ques-tioning, plus (LGBTQ+) orientations, which must also be considered by leaders. It was not until 2020 that the U.S. Supreme Court offered a minimum level of protection by ruling that the Civil Rights Act of 1964 protected gay, les-bian, and transgender employees from discrimination based on sex. That's one heck of a long time for anyone to wait for legal protection, let alone a group that makes up an estimated 5 percent of all working adults.

"Stigma-related prejudice and discrimination experienced by LGBTQ people constitute chronically stressful events that can lead to negative health outcomes," said Cathy Kelle-her of the Technological University Dublin. Her research has found that bias-related stress has been linked to psychologi-cal distress among gay men and lesbian women. In fact, re-search shows as high as 60 percent of LGBTQ+ people deal with anxiety and depression at some point in their lives—a rate two and a half times higher than their heterosexual counterparts.

Brad Brenner, PhD, a counseling psychologist, says: "If you're LGBTQ, I'd wager a bet that you're really good at reading a situation to determine how much you can safely be yourself. This skill comes at a cost because it was developed in response to being subjected to high levels of persistent prejudice and discrimination. Many people come to view themselves as deeply flawed, unlovable, unworthy, and hopeless."

Psychologists refer to this process of dealing as "minority stress," and studies show it has powerful, lasting impacts on mental health and well-being—intensified for those struggling with anxiety. Stigma is a significant issue. If an employee can't talk about who they are at their core, there's a likelihood they will feel greater levels of anxiety and unease every day.

In our interview with branding author Dorie Clark, who has written extensively on LGBTQ+ issues for the *Harvard Business Review*, she explained, "The stress around hiding can become extraordinarily distracting, leaving people less energy for their work. As anybody who's ever been in junior high knows, when you have to focus too much on what people are thinking about you, it's a surefire recipe for anxiety."

She added that managers can help dispel such worries. Putting antidiscrimination policies in place is fundamental, but beyond that team leaders can speak up for marginalized groups, initiate inclusion conversations with their teams, and treat all complaints as serious (even about seemingly minor issues) and investigate them immediately.

"Humans are highly calibrated to pick up on signals from

other humans. If you are concealing something, other people generally know it," Clark added. "They might not know what it is, but they know you seem guarded. Saying you are gay—or whatever one's identity is—is usually the most innocuous explanation because people might concoct a million bad things: This person's a snob, or they think they are superior, or, worse, they are doing something wrong and don't want us to know about it."

Hiding our true identities isn't just an issue for those in the LGBTQ+ community. The Deloitte University Leadership Center reveals that 61 percent of all employees say they hide part of their identity in some way. For instance, a working mom might not talk about her kids to appear more "serious" about her career; a Muslim employee might have to find a hidden corner of the office to pray so no one will see him; or a gay man might not display pictures of his partner at work or even on social media.

When managers create cultures where people feel comfortable being themselves, dramatic performance gains can be unlocked as everyone is able to focus all their attention on work. Whether or not they are part of a traditional minority group, team leaders should be able to share at least one story of identity-covering in their own behavior to display vulnerability.

Please note that in all this, no one wants to be defined by a single dimension of their identity, e.g., "the Black guy" or "the gay teammate." That also means managers should not ask individuals to give opinions representing their entire group.

LGBTQ+, Muslim, or Black people are not a monolith. After all, no one would think to ask something like: "Jerry, you are White; what would White people think about this product?" Managers can help by recognizing that everyone has differences, and those parts of us represent only a fraction of who we are.

Oh, and in all of this, nothing ever gives managers permission to "out" people who aren't ready.

I Don't See Color
(and Other Dumb Things to Say)

Howard Schultz, former CEO of Starbucks, said at a town-hall event that he doesn't see color when it comes to race. Schultz said, "As somebody who grew up in a very diverse background as a young boy in the projects, I didn't see color as a young boy and I honestly don't see color now."

Says activist Franchesca Ramsey, "People who say this usually mean well—they want you to know they're *sooo* not racist that they can't even conceive of a reality in which racism exists. But what they're actually saying is that racial *identity* is bad, not that racial *oppression* is bad. It suggests people's experiences aren't valid—or flat-out aren't real. If you wear glasses and I say, 'I don't even see your glasses,' that doesn't mean you suddenly have 20/20 vision; it just means I'm in denial. Or maybe I need glasses myself."

Statements denying there's a problem are problematic to diversity and inclusion efforts, says Janice Gassam, PhD, author of *Dirty Diversity.* "Anyone who is able to see can discern and recognize one skin color from the next. How can you possibly fix something that you don't believe you actually see? It's important to understand that the goal is not to be color-blind. The goal is actually to see and recognize skin color but to control and regulate your innate impulse to make decisions based on such characteristics," she added.

Gassam is of course correct. We all see color. We see height and weight. We remember when someone tells us they are part of the LGBTQ+ community or a minority religious group. We must recognize that each of us has preconceived notions and expectations about different groups of people. Pretending we can't see differences shows a lack of empathy and ignores when certain groups or individuals are being alienated. Implicit bias is something that we shouldn't be afraid to recognize in ourselves, and we should actually seek it out so we can unlearn expectations.

Two of the leading scholars in implicit bias, social psychologists Mahzarin R. Banaji and Anthony G. Greenwald, talk about this in their aptly titled book *Blindspot: Hidden Biases of Good People.* They say implicit bias can affect people who say, quite honestly, that they are horrified by these types of attitudes. They refer to a study by the Pew Research Center. Using a computerized speed test, researchers found only 20 percent of Asian American adult test-takers and only 30 percent of White adults participating did not exhibit any subconscious racial preference between White people and Asian people. When measuring preference between White people and Black people, only 27 percent of White adults and 26 percent of Black adults showed no implicit bias.

In one version of this test, researchers took famous Asian Americans such as Connie Chung, Michael Chang, and Kristi Yamaguchi and White foreigners such as Hugh Grant, Katarina Witt, and Gerard Depardieu, and timed test-takers connecting them to American symbols and foreign symbols. They learned that people found it much easier to associate Hugh Grant with American symbols than Connie Chung. "That shows how deeply the category 'American' is White in many people's minds," Banaji said.

Implicit biases developed from a human need to process information quickly to make split-second decisions; the brain is constantly using shortcuts to find connections between bits of data that come our way. If we are crossing the road, for instance, and we see a moving blur in the corner of our vision, our brains will very quickly connect that with an approaching car and we'll jump. Life saved. Unfortunately, implicit biases can lead to harmful stereotypes when applied to people. As just one example, women are too often subconsciously perceived as less capable in traditionally male roles, say computer programming. A woman might pick up on her interviewer's hesitancy and begin to feel less confident in herself, throwing the interview off course.

Despite our best intentions, and without our awareness, stereotypes and assumptions can very easily creep into our minds and affect our actions, even when we are completely determined to be objective and fair. It is so prevalent that

20 percent of large US companies today provide implicit bias trainings to their employees, and half of US companies say they will offer it within the next few years. Starbucks recently closed all of its stores to have mandatory racial bias training for its employees. That's a good start. When biases are not addressed, they can affect working relationships and trust, undercut diverse talent recruitment and inclusion efforts, and impact promotion and professional development opportunities.

Derek Lundsten, president and CEO of LifeGuides, believes being different should be a good thing. "You don't have to be a person of color or of a certain identity or a certain gender to feel on the outside. In an organization, part of what we, as leaders, need to create is an environment where our differences are celebrated. That's what makes work interesting, exciting—the different approaches, ideas, and backgrounds."

As we spoke with individuals in marginalized communities, a few things they wanted managers to understand about addressing bias included: 1) Don't try to convince a person from a marginalized group of all the things that have gone wrong in your life to better relate to their issues (you were poor, your parents died, you have a learning disorder, etc.); this is not a competition. 2) Don't ante up by saying that your daughter is gay or that you have lots of Black friends. 3) Be compassionate but don't be "shocked" by racism or other forms of bias; if you are, you have been actively ignoring what's been happening because it did not affect you directly. 4) Don't preach about your "wokeness" to the issue; show it (we'll get to how in a minute).

Says Katie Burke, chief people officer for HubSpot, "Allyship is a verb, and it starts with a combination of self-awareness and empathy. You have to adopt a mindset where you're constantly learning, growing, and improving how you stand up and show up for others. It's a lifelong commitment to building relationships based on trust, consistency, and accountability with marginalized individuals or groups."

It's our responsibility as leaders to ensure those who are in need of support aren't left feeling like they're alone, added Terry Jackson, PhD, an executive coach and CEO of the Jackson Consulting Group. "Every day, your employees deal with social issues. Those issues will impact productivity and the level of engagement within your organization. If you're an emotionally intelligent leader, you understand what is going on in the community that's impacting your vulnerable employees. If you are not embracing those issues, discussing them and trying to solve them, you're going to end up on the wrong side of history because we are at the tipping point where everybody is willing to engage around what is right for humanity."

Fundamentally, to do what Jackson suggests, leaders must start by believing people when they say they are hurt by racism, sexism, or other forms of discrimination. The Black Lives Matter protests of 2020, for instance, didn't spring up out of nowhere. They exposed a nerve that has long been ignored in America, that we are a nation still divided by inequality. As leaders who care about our people—their lives and emotional experiences—we need to be there for each other. After all, being the "only" in any group can be lonely and isolating, especially when no one speaks up for you, when no one believes the challenges you face every day.

"As more and more companies attempt to build more diverse and inclusive workforces, one of the dynamics that fundamentally needs to shift is who speaks up on matters of belonging," said Burke of HubSpot.

Who is that? The leader.

Real Leadership

Rosabeth Moss Kanter, professor at Harvard Business School, said, "It takes courage to speak up against complacency and injustice while others remain silent. But that's what leadership is." The sad truth is we expect people who are underrepresented to speak up for themselves about injustices. Often, colleagues and managers don't believe them. Worse, they get combative. As leaders, we don't spend nearly enough time thinking about how to address the microaggressions that happen every day in our workplaces that affect marginalized people deeply.

As a definition, microaggressions are biases that reveal themselves in often subtle ways and leave people feeling uncomfortable or insulted. They may range from the offensive—a Black man notices a lone White woman flinch when he steps into the elevator, or a woman tries to speak up in a meeting but can't get a word in with her male colleagues—to the bizarre—a gay man is told that he must love a certain musician, or a person in a wheelchair is jokily told to "slow down, speed racer." We had a young friend explain that during her time as a teaching assistant at a local university, her professor would introduce her to the class with comments such as "I want you all to enjoy the lecture, so here's a pretty face." She knew it wasn't meant to be harmful, but the comments ratcheted up her anxiety considerably and made her unsure of her abilities. She was, in fact, a qualified researcher and lecturer, but the professor's comments framed her first as a thing to ogle. Instead, think of how engaged our friend would have been if the professor had bookended her lecture time with glowing comments about her research and educational accomplishments.

This kind of death-by-a-thousand-cuts behavior is brushed off too frequently with those on the receiving end being termed "overly sensitive." Yet research shows that microaggressions can take a real psychological toll on the mental health of recipients, may lead to anger and depression, and can lower work productivity and problem-solving abilities. One study at Marquette University provided strong evidence that microaggressions lead not only to elevated levels of depression and trauma, but thoughts of suicide in those affected.

What follows are a few methods offered to us by powerful voices in marginalized communities and their allies to help those who feel on the outside become valued and included in any team.

Method 1: Listen Up

"If someone is brave and courageous enough to share their unique experience and perspective with you, honor it. Amplify it. Create space for it in your team meetings, in your business, and in your brand," said HubSpot's Burke. This means listening to those experiences.

Evelyn Walter, executive director and HR leader for Cummins engine and power generation business in North American distribution, sought to listen following the 2020 Black Lives Matter protests. A Fortune 500 company with sixty thousand employees around the world, Cummins has six core values, one of which is diversity and inclusion. Thus, when the marches began, Walter told us she felt supported by her organization to send a handwritten card to every Black person on her staff.

"I got approval to use home addresses, and I wrote lengthy notes about how I wanted to support them," she said. "I asked what I could do for them and their families. I was in the car Friday with my husband and daughters and got an email from a woman named Mercedes. She is incredibly positive; she makes lemonade out of lemons every day. The main message was she appreciated the specific care for her and her family. She said, 'I've seen your leadership, I know this is sincere.' That was kind, and yet it was concerning because she obviously knows other people who may not be genuine."

Added Walter, the act of writing out dozens of notes on a Saturday morning spurred her to create further connections. "I wanted to find more people to check in with. What about my Latinx employees? What about my team members who are gay? That's what it created in me."

HubSpot's Burke added to this idea. She has served as the

LGBTQ+ executive sponsor at her firm, but didn't feel she knew much about the experience of folks who identify as transgender and how she could best support them. She spent time researching the issue, and hours listening to colleagues she admired who identify as transgender. In doing so she learned more about preferred pronoun usage, the transition process, and how she could be a more supportive colleague, friend, and leader.

Admitting you don't know all the answers and being vulnerable enough to address your blind spots proactively is a vital part of the role of anyone who wishes to be an ally. Yes, most of us will make a mistake or two in this process—we are all human—but through listening and education we will start to understand how to better help all those whose lives we touch.

Method 2: Sponsor

Karen Catlin, author of *Better Allies* and former vice president of engineering at Adobe, told of working early in her career for a software company that was acquired by a larger firm. "In the first few months following the acquisition, I noticed something. My new manager, Digby Horner—who had been at the larger company for many years—said things in meetings along the lines of: 'What I learned from Karen is . . .' By doing this, Digby helped me build credibility with my new colleagues. He took action as an ally, using his position of privilege to sponsor me. His shout-outs made a difference, and definitely made me feel great."

What we learn from this is twofold. First, Digby Horner is probably the coolest name ever. And second, more on point, when allies take on the role of sponsor, they vocally support the work of colleagues from underrepresented groups in all contexts, specifically in situations that will help boost their reputation. This can't be pandering but has to be honest promotion of people's expertise.

The goal for leaders is to support and promote those from oft-marginalized groups. For example, for several years Adrian has been asked to deliver keynotes on corporate culture at the Women's Foodservice Forum, an industry group with the goal of advancing female leaders in foodservice. Three thousand attendees arrive each year to hear messages from luminaries such as Brené Brown and Maya Angelou. Adrian has been inspired by those attending and found it significant that about 10 percent of the attendees are senior male leaders—there to learn and champion the women in their organizations to greater success. These men are not benevolent benefactors, but wise leaders who intentionally invest in and rely on the skills of their protégés to achieve greater things for their organizations.

Method 3: Stand Up

Good allies don't hide in the shadows, says Isaac Sabat, assistant professor of organizational psychology at Texas A&M University. Instead, they show their support through actions, even by seemingly small things like attending events, adding comments on Slack, or affixing stickers to their cubicles. He said, "Research shows that confronting bad behavior in the moment—responding to someone's insensitive remark or calling attention to the lack of representation in the room—can be more effective when it comes from an ally." If a person of color, for instance, calls out a microaggression, other teammates might see them as complaining or self-serving, he added, but when allies initiate a similar confrontation, others typically view it as objective.

"If you can signal your allyship identity, then it shows people that you are supportive and that you are there for them if something goes down." Yet Sabat notes that stepping up once isn't enough, and allyship is a journey that grows throughout a leader's career. "Be open to criticism and feedback," he adds. "If someone calls you out on the way you [respond to a situation], or if you said something problematic, be open to learning and growing."

Method 4: Advocate

Susan Wojcicki, CEO of YouTube, says addressing imbalances requires those who have power and influence to extend their privilege. For instance, she says, "In every organization, there are many people—from senior leaders to first-time managers—who have the power to elevate women in the workplace." One of those who advocated for Wojcicki was Bill Campbell, executive coach to a who's-who of tech superstars. "I learned about an important invitation-only conference convening most of the top leaders in tech and media, yet my name was left off the guest list," she said. "Many of the invitees were my peers [other tech CEOs], meaning that You-Tube wouldn't be represented while deals were cut and plans were made. I started to question whether I even belonged at the conference. But rather than let it go, I turned to Bill, someone I knew had a lot of influence. He immediately recognized I had a rightful place at the event, and within a day he worked his magic and I received my invitation."

When allies assume the role of advocates, they use their influence to bring peers from underrepresented groups into new circles. They hold their leadership peers accountable for including qualified colleagues of all genders, races and ethnicities, abilities, ages, body shapes and sizes, religions, and sexual orientations; and they actively mentor those from underrepresented groups and introduce them to people in their network. This means they aren't just behind-the-scenes mentors, but public advocates for those they are mentoring. They find terrific satisfaction in identifying high-potential diverse talent, providing them stretch roles, and helping them overcome obstacles. They find this kind of mentoring behavior is good not only for the protégé, but for the leader and the organization.

SUMMARY

- There has been a historic pattern of anxiety in particular groups within the workplace—those too often made to feel like "others." Of particular concern are women, people of color, those on the LGBTQ+ spectrum, members of religious minorities, and those with disabilities.

- Many in these communities must hide their true identities. But when managers create cultures where people feel comfortable being themselves, dramatic performance gains can be unlocked as everyone is able to focus all their attention on work.

- Many leaders do not understand the level of implicit bias that occurs in our work cultures. Microaggressions are biases that reveal themselves in often subtle ways and leave people feeling uncomfortable or insulted. They can take a psychological toll on the mental health of recipients and can lower work productivity and problem-solving abilities.

- Methods to help those who are marginalized feel valued and included in any team include: 1) listen up, 2) sponsor, 3) stand up, and 4) advocate.

Transform Exclusion into Connection

HELP TEAM MEMBERS BUILD SOCIAL BONDS

The greatest kindness is acceptance.

—Christina Baker Kline, novelist

In some fascinating work done at Cornell University, researchers found that fire stations perform better—including saving more lives—when firefighters eat meals as a team. "Eating together is a more intimate act than looking over an Excel spreadsheet together. That intimacy spills over into work," said the study's lead author, Dr. Kevin Kniffin. In fact, the researchers noted that firefighters in stations where everyone dined alone often expressed embarrassment when asked why. "It was basically a signal that something deeper was wrong with the way the group worked," Kniffin said.

Eating together for firefighters is a big sign that everyone is accepted. We are not suggesting every team needs to run out to Chili's at noon every day, but after twenty years of working with organizations around the world, we can attest that finding ways to include everyone can create boons to team performance. In contrast, exclusion can lead to job dissatisfaction and higher employee turnover.

We've probably all been left out at some point in our lives; it evokes unpleasant memories from school playground days. While much has been written on bullying at work as a serious concern for employees' mental health and team cohesion, research shows exclusion can be just as toxic to anxiety levels and hasn't received anywhere near the attention. FOMO and being excluded at work can cast a dark shadow on one's life, suggests Professor Sandra Robinson of the University of British Columbia. This is because we as humans have such a strong need to belong. Robinson's research indicates that 71 percent of professionals say they have experienced some degree of exclusion from their team—even before the coronavirus pandemic isolated so many. And ostracism in the workplace can have long-term psychological implications, she adds.

Exclusion can impact anyone and be a huge contributor to anxiety. As leaders, a step forward in inclusion awareness is to understand that when team members shun or snub other employees, it can make those people feel like they're not fully accepted or respected by their colleagues. These actions are often insidious and subtle: phone calls that are not returned, meetings where some are not invited, lunch offers that never come. Ostracism like this not only affects morale; it can affect an individual's productivity and a team's ability to hit its goals.

What's Not Happening . . . and What Is

In some cases, exclusion is not intentional; and inadvertent actions can be tricky to spot. They are sins of omission: the result of help *not* offered, conversations *not* engaged in, camaraderie *not* shared. How are managers supposed to see what's *not* happening?

There's actually quite a lot that team leaders can do to encourage inclusion; for instance, looking carefully for anyone on the team who may seem to be left out (all the more important when some or all of a team works remotely), which person is regularly cut off during group discussions, who is regularly chatting with whom, and who doesn't seem to be interacting with anyone. By watching, a manager can gain awareness and insight. But regular one-on-ones are probably the best way to understand what's really going on: asking about people's interactions with others on the team and if they are having challenges with any specific personalities.

At FYidoctors, doctors and team leaders follow what they call a Ten-Ten Commitment in their optometry clinics, labs, and home office departments. "For the first ten minutes of each day, leaders walk around and ask their team members how they are doing with a friendly hello and no other agenda but a welcome to the day," said president Darcy Verhun. "It's incumbent on the leaders to do this to demonstrate visible leadership and caring. It's ten minutes at the start of the day, and another ten minutes at the end of the day to see how everyone's day has gone. I'm amazed at the power of a simple check-in."

Verhun added, "These check-ins are not so that the team can hear the leader's story, but so the leaders can hear their team members' stories and connect. We have received such positive feedback from the team on this leadership commitment and have found it reduces anxiety."

But even if managers pick up on exclusion, they still need specific approaches to help their people move from feeling isolated to connected and accepted. We are not necessarily suggesting dragging everyone out for karaoke or starting a potluck Friday, but a few ideas that can help immediately include:

+ Ensure that all team members can contribute in meetings and have their voices heard in a calm, organized manner.

+ Buddy new hires up with more seasoned employees who they might form a connection with (*friendly* seasoned employees, that is).

+ Spend time in every meeting recognizing the contributions of individuals as well as those of the group as a whole.

+ Go out of the way to make remote workers feel fully accepted—e.g., even though some people may be working in the office, now and then ask everyone to join meetings via electronic means. Also bring remote people into the workplace on a regular basis.

What follows are a few more methods used by leaders we've interviewed and worked with to enhance inclusion and strengthen bonds in their teams to great effect.

Method 1: Build Camaraderie

Ryan Westwood, CEO of Simplus, told us that he was affected when conducting a one-on-one with a remote employee via teleconference during the pandemic. "She said to me, in tears, 'I haven't had a hug in three months.' Her grown boys live in different states. My heart was breaking. We have to be conscious of our coworkers and their situations, more than ever when people are working remotely."

As such, his company has created geographic regions for its six hundred employees. In areas with at least ten people, employees are given a budget to do "service projects, go bowling, do whatever you want to do." Westwood added, "We don't have a leader looming over the gatherings. It's about people genuinely connecting in the way they want. We have found that our employee happiness and employee net promoter scores have gone way up from this small budget."

In another of our clients, a new team was formed during a reorganization. The group consisted of people who had not worked together before, who had various backgrounds and experiences. They were to provide support services to several divisions of the company, meaning they would be gone from the office most of their days. The leader knew this environment could be ripe for feelings of exclusion and anxiety, so she initiated a few simple activities that built esprit de corps and fostered inclusion.

She brought the team together in the office first thing every Thursday morning without fail to see how the work was going, analyze loads and balance tasks, and brainstorm ways to help each other (these moved to teleconferences during the pandemic). She kept the meetings to an hour, and made sure no one voice dominated, yet no one was allowed to stay quiet either. To be respectful to those who may be anxious about speaking in public, and so no one would feel *pushed* onto a stage, she spent a few minutes the day before putting together an agenda, letting each team member know the specific updates she would ask them to share with the group. Not only did this make her more introverted workers feel more at ease with their part in the discussion—as they had time to prepare—the whole meeting ran more smoothly.

During the sessions, she followed a round-robin format, in which everyone got a chance to share their thoughts in turn. Her meetings may not have had the chaotic excitement of some brainstorming sessions, but her anxious people felt included and safe to speak up in this calm setting, leading to a tremendous amount of creative ideas flowing from the group.

The team also started handing around a traveling trophy in those meetings, in this case a bowling loving cup the manager had bought at a Goodwill store. It was awarded by one team member to another in recognition of the other's contribution to rolling up sleeves and helping out during the week. The new recipient then had a week to decide who would receive the trophy next. The effect: It caused everyone to come to the Thursday meeting asking themselves if they'd done enough to help other team members, and they got to consider all the things that others on the team had done to help them.

The leader also initiated rules to help enhance inclusion. For example, all emails between team members would be responded to within twenty-four hours (Monday to Friday), team members wouldn't interrupt each other during discussions, and the group would commit to a no-meeting Friday schedule (so they could get work done or use vacation time). Finally, knowing that many of her new team members might stress about how they were performing in this new setting, she spent time at the end of each day sending specific feedback notes to her people to help them know that she knew about the work they were doing and valued their contributions.

One of her employees we interviewed told us that within just a few weeks, he felt bonded to his new team members. He also said that while in prior teams he had been focused almost exclusively on his own performance, he was now considering daily how he could contribute to the overall success of the group. The thoughtful inclusion tactics by the manager helped anyone feel that they were valued as part of the team.

Method 2: Find a Common Core

For teams we are asked to work with that are struggling to mesh strong personalities, we find the journey from exclusion to connection can be complex and has to be founded on shared values.

We had a chance to interview Mitt Romney not long after he retired from Bain Capital and before his election as

Massachusetts governor and his run for president. We were most interested in his work helping launch the investment firm that today has more than $100 billion under management. He confessed that at one point in its early days, the Bain Capital partners were eyeing the door with what he called "intractable conflicts." In a last-ditch effort to save the firm, six of the founders agreed to attend a weeklong program that reportedly had helped other teams. "It was worth a try," Romney recalled.

The extent of the team dysfunction became evident in one of the early sessions. Each member was asked to openly and honestly describe the things he would change in each of the other individuals. The "targets" were not permitted to reply or defend themselves. The session was scheduled to last an hour, but their kvetching not only took the entire evening, it spilled over into the next morning and set "new records in inventive criticism," Romney said.

Despite the counseling, the group neared the end of the retreat wondering if they could ever work together. Then a final, one-hour exercise changed everything.

In that session, the instructor taught the group that if individuals live in conflict with their core values, they will be unhappy, unhealthy, and less successful. In psychology, that is called cognitive dissonance, when people experience stress from holding contradictory beliefs or when they engage in actions that go against their values. Internal conflict between how one lives and what one values creates stress, and the consequences of stress can be dire. Further, the instructor taught, if individuals in a group have widely divergent core values, it will be very hard for the group to work together inclusively.

"I thought I had my answer as to why our team was disintegrating: Our values were miles apart," Romney said. "One partner said his life ambition was to be in the *Forbes* list of wealthiest people, another wanted fame and recognition to compensate for his life's early indignities, and another cared primarily about his family life. Our instructor said that it was possible that our actual core values weren't that disparate. Instead, it might be that what we were working for, saying to ourselves that we wanted from life, was in conflict with our own core values."

The instructor asked the group to list the five people they most respected—living or dead. Then next to each person's name they wrote the three characteristics they most associated with that individual. Romney made his list of people and chose words and phrases to describe them. They were: "service," "love of others," "integrity," "faith," "compassion," "vision," "strength of character."

Finally, group members were instructed to select the three words that appeared most frequently on their lists. Romney's words were "love," "service," and "faith."

"I wondered what my partners' lists would show," Romney says. He was surprised. "We had all arrived at basically the same values. Every one of us had included love and service. And in the list of people we most admired, every one of us had included Abraham Lincoln.

"We were not so different after all," he concludes.

The partners realized they needed to align their team's mission with its members' core values, then work together with a keen focus on those ideals.

"I can't say that our business suddenly transformed into an enterprise of love and service," Romney says. "But I *can* say that it changed, and we changed, too. We worked together, relatively productively, for another ten years, for which I give a good measure of credit to what we discovered about ourselves that day."

Method 3: Foster Connections and Friendships

As we often see with high-powered, high-salary sports teams, not everyone has to like the people they work with to be successful. But, since we spend more time at work than anywhere else, it certainly makes things a lot more pleasant when we do all get along.

We have to understand, however, that not everyone may feel comfortable in social settings—especially people with anxiety. Traditional activities intended to bring teams together were typically designed by extroverts, for extroverts. Even the idea of open-space offices was most definitely not discussed with any introverts before launch. Yet we've found there's much leaders can do to encourage the quiet and shy to join in on a little socializing without going to extremes.

For instance, instead of having people work by themselves on every project, we've seen team leaders create more opportunities for assignments to be completed in groups of two or more—even if people are remote. Encouraging the group to get together outside of work to do charity work, do something active, or attend a conference is another good way to encourage inclusion that's less anxiety-inducing than just looking at each other across a table at a restaurant—since people are focused on an activity.

Derek Lundsten and Stephan Vincent lead an online network, LifeGuides, that gives people peer-to-peer connections like this. Peers help peers through life's challenges, from anxiety at work to dealing with COVID-19 to social justice. Companies like Salesforce.com and The Motley Fool offer the platform to their employees. Said Vincent, "In life, we get overloaded with information from various sources and the world is very polarizing. I've experienced it with family members. When you get into a topic—COVID-19, the economy, whatever—suddenly it becomes political, polarizing, and you don't get the support you were looking for. Therapists and other professionals may be helpful but see things through a medical lens. When you create a connection with someone who's been in your shoes, they can understand and empathize and provide guidance. Then you build human relationships that can help."

Emma Seppälä and Marissa King of Yale University note that "people who have a 'best friend at work' are not only more likely to be happier and healthier, they are also seven times as likely to be engaged in their job. What's more, employees who report having friends at work have higher levels of productivity, retention, and job satisfaction than those who don't." Of course, friendships in the office can be tricky.

As a note: Team members' interpersonal relationships are typically none of our business as managers; that is, until team performance is impacted. When taken to extremes, for instance, cliquishness can create *Survivor*-like alliances and tribes that can cause more exclusion for some. Also, when boundaries are blurred between the professional and the personal, there's an opportunity for feelings and group performance to be hurt. However, the fact that there is potential for entanglements is not an excuse for managers to avoid connecting employees with each other. Workers don't necessarily have to go out for drinks or share intimate personal details about themselves, e.g., *So that's the story of my lower back tattoo*. No, positive relationships are built on vulnerability, authenticity, and compassion—and those can happen within work hours, within healthy boundaries (such as establishing rules about avoiding office gossip and that everyone should be included and treated equally). Managers should also model those behaviors in their interactions with their team members, say Seppälä and King.

So, should managers try to be friends with those they supervise? While they can be warm and caring, managers should not be too chummy with their employees. We could point (as a bad example) to the wayward wisdom of Michael Scott of *The Office*, who was so concerned with being his employees' best friend that he couldn't hold anyone accountable. "Would I rather be feared or loved? Easy: both. I want people to be afraid of how much they love me," he said. Though entertaining, no one should ever attempt to emulate Scott's behavior in the workplace, or anywhere else.

We were once asked to coach a high-potential manager. The division director admitted he'd promoted the fellow to a supervisory position because, in addition to being competent in his finance role, he got along with everyone. "He was the guy you'd most want to go to a party with," said the director. But once Mr. Life of the Office became the "boss," he became Mr. Tough Guy. What friendships had existed became frayed. No one wanted to even have a casual conversation with him. It seemed like all he could talk about was deadlines and quotas, and his constant scowl seemed to show his team members they weren't doing all they could. It took considerable coaching, as well as some pretty blunt 360-degree feedback, to get him to see the light, that he'd gone too far and was adding significantly to the team's anxiety levels.

In another case, we were asked to work with a leader who had come from outside the organization to assume a senior role over a team that needed some direction. She told us she'd never been big on conflict. "I expect my employees to do their jobs without hand-holding," she said in our first session. In 360s with her team, we heard several complaints that her new employees didn't know where they really stood with her. Everything was hinted at. "Become a better coach" and "become more assertive" were the two leadership skills we worked with her on over the coming months.

Executive coach Peter Bregman had a similar experience with two of his clients. One of them was seen as the apparent successor to the CEO, but he had a problem. "Several of his direct reports were close friends, and he didn't hold them accountable in the same way he held his other direct reports," said Bregman. "They didn't do what he asked and weren't delivering the results expected. It was hurting his business and his reputation."

Bregman said the other members of this team saw the problem clearly enough and they admitted it was affecting their own motivation because of the unfairness. The leader, on the other hand, had blinders on. He didn't see it.

Bregman's other client was CEO of a fast-growing billion-dollar enterprise. "He's warm, gregarious, and authentic," said the coach. "He's learned, the hard way, that having friends when you're the boss can be complicated."

He used to have work friends come to his house for dinner and get to know his family. "But then I had to make hard calls for the good of the business, including firing one of them, and it became too painful. I became hesitant to make decisions because of it. So no, I'm not looking for friends at work."

Bregman explained that this second leader doesn't avoid friendships with employees because he is a *bad* guy. He avoids them because he is a *good* guy. Indeed, it can be hard for leaders to have close friends in the employee ranks, either because they can't separate friendships from business decisions, or because they have to make tough calls that may destroy those relationships.

"There's plenty of research supporting the idea that having friends at work makes you happier and more engaged," Bregman adds. "But the research doesn't address that friendships at work are tricky, especially when you're the boss."

This means for those who are promoted from individual contributor to manager, or from manager to a manager-of-managers, they can choose to be proactive. Says Professor Art Markman of the University of Texas at Austin, "Make an effort to take some of your [work] friends out and talk to them about some of the stresses and responsibilities of the new position. Help them understand some of the tensions you're feeling. You may assume that your friends will implicitly understand the tensions you have, but they are much more likely to be sympathetic if you have an open conversation."

Method 4: Provide Frequent Validation

What else can a manager do to facilitate feelings of connection and avoid exclusion in their teams? We turn to a commencement address given at Harvard University by Oprah Winfrey: "I have to say that the single most important lesson I learned in twenty-five years talking every single day to people was that there's a common denominator in our human experience: We want to be validated. We want to be understood. I've done over thirty-five thousand interviews in my career. And as soon as that camera shuts off, everyone turns to me and inevitably, in their own way, asks this question: 'Was that okay?' I heard it from President Bush. I heard it from President Obama. I've heard it from heroes and from housewives. I've heard it from victims and perpetrators of crimes. I even heard it from Beyoncé in all of her Beyoncéness. . . . [We] all want to know, 'Did you hear me? Do you see me? Did what I say mean anything to you?'"

What Winfrey speaks about is a leader noticing and appreciating a person's inherent value. That's part of gratitude, which we'll dive into more in Chapter 9. The point of gratitude isn't just about thanking others for their accomplishments, it's about helping people see their worth as a colleague and a human being. And it pays off for managers, too. In one Glassdoor survey, more than half of employees said feeling more appreciation from their boss would help them stay longer at their company.

Method 5: Include Remotes

A last suggestion in the process of fighting exclusion is to carefully include those who work remotely all or part of the time, which can certainly be anxiety-inducing in and of itself. One of the growing effects of the COVID-19 pandemic is that more organizations have embraced the concept of working from home. Before the virus, most of our clients had a small percent of people who worked away from the office. Some were allowing their people to work a day a week remotely. Then the virus came and overnight everyone had to learn to work off-site.

Some companies have realized this can have distinctive advantages. Commute time disappears, meetings grow shorter and can be more focused, they can access talent from anywhere in the world, and many have been able to downsize physical facilities. One of those companies is a telecom firm we share office space with. Leaders decided to permanently shutter an office and have their people work from home. We bumped into some of the IT professionals and they acted as if they'd been given a second Christmas. *I don't have to deal with people interrupting me anymore!* In contrast, some of the bubbly client services folks acted as if the world was about to end considering that they would not be together in person day-to-day.

After twenty years of helping define and refine corporate culture, we can offer up one warning: Most businesses took their corporate cultures for granted when all employees worked in the same building. When considering the world of remote work, we are entering the Wild West. Helping people—perhaps spread out over various time zones—feel like a part of a collective whole is an entirely different matter.

To build culture in a remote world, and reduce anxiety in the process, managers must communicate more, not less, to help their people feel included and not be afraid to try to break out of the status quo. Kraft Heinz Company has done just that. Shirley Weinstein, head of Global Rewards, shared that her executive team has participated in live cooking showdowns in their home kitchens for employees to watch—incorporating their products from Philadelphia Cream Cheese to Oscar Mayer to Classico Pasta Sauce. The half-hour shows pit two executives against each other, cooking in their kitchens in front of their families. "Our global head of communications, Michael Mullen, is the engaging moderator, with a member of our culinary team to judge the creativity and use of our products," she said. "The taste testers are their families, which is a great way to bring their children, their spouses, and even their dogs into the show."

She added that busy employees working remotely at first thought, "'I don't have time for this,' but they joined in and appreciated the diversity that it brought to their workday. It was a time to reflect, to learn, to laugh, and to appreciate their leaders on a personal level."

As Kraft Heinz is attempting, building culture in a remote world also means clearly defining your mission and values and celebrating those who embody these grand ideals in interactions with customers or fellow team members. It also means using technology platforms and social media to provide ways that employees can connect and get to know each other, replicating the old water-cooler talk or sticking your head over the cubicle wall.

Managers with remote teams also should spread leadership around to enhance ownership and engagement—asking certain folks on the team to run meetings about a subject they are passionate about or conduct training sessions on an area of their expertise. Bosses can also bring some fun into the mix by encouraging home workspace decorating contests or background competitions. Even little things can help build connection. For instance, if leaders bring in lunch for people who are in the office, they can make sure to send food to remote people as well. That's a nice touch.

Beth Schinoff of Boston College and Blake Ashforth and Kevin Corley of Arizona State University say that remote work is changing how we relate to our coworkers in two important ways. First, employees are going to become less likely to live close to their coworkers. "This means that we may not have the opportunity for in-person, informal shared experiences . . . as well as organizationally sponsored shared experiences." Second, workers will increasingly rely on technology to communicate with colleagues versus face-to-face interactions. Interacting through media like text, instant message, and even teleconferences can make it harder to get a sense of who someone is. "We can't assess body language and other nonlinguistic cues in the same way we can in-person," the authors say. "When we work via technology, it is also more likely that we will only communicate with our virtual coworkers when we have a reason to."

Given these fundamental differences in how we relate when working virtually, how *do* remote colleagues gain the friendships that are necessary to enhance engagement and loyalty, not to mention drive better outcomes? Schinoff and her colleagues advocate developing a cadence.

"Remote workers feel like they have cadence with a coworker when they understand who that person is and can predict how they will interact," they write. "Cadence is especially important when we work virtually because it helps us anticipate *when* we will [need to] interact with our virtual coworkers and *how* those interactions will go, things that are much easier to do when communicating face-to-face. When we don't have cadence with our coworkers, we might find it difficult to get in contact with them or find it frustrating to interact with them when we do."

What can leaders and managers do to establish such a cadence when their people are remote? This involves setting the stage for employees to get to know each other. But instead of asking team members to introduce themselves, which can be anxiety-inducing, roundabout ways can produce better results. For instance, one manager had employees share a song with their teammates that they had enjoyed listening to in the past week; another asked her people to share something off their bucket list. The spotlight moment became more about how awesome Marvin Gaye's "What's Going On" is, or why Machu Picchu would be so cool to visit, than about the person; yet these quick sidelights gave tons of insights into the employee's personality. Another simple idea: Opening telecom lines ten minutes before a team conference call and leaving them open for ten minutes after so that team members can chat if they'd like.

Build Social Bonds

- Exclusion can be toxic to anxiety levels. Fear of missing out (FOMO) may harm mental well-being since humans have such a strong need to belong. Some 71 percent of professionals say they have experienced some degree of exclusion within their team.

- There is much team leaders can do to spot those who may seem to be left out—all the more important when some or all of a team works remotely: Which person is regularly cut off during group discussions? Who doesn't seem to be interacting with anyone? Regular one-on-ones are the best way to understand what's really going on.

- Leaders can encourage inclusion by ensuring that all team members can contribute in meetings and have their voices heard in a calm and organized manner, buddy new hires up with friendly seasoned employees, and spend time in every meeting recognizing contributions.

- Other methods for helping move a team from exclusion to connection include: 1) build camaraderie, 2) find a common core, 3) foster connections and friendships, 4) provide frequent validation, and 5) include remotes.

Turn Doubts into Assurance

HOW GRATITUDE CAN HELP TEAM MEMBERS BUILD CONFIDENCE

The way to develop what's best that is in a person is by appreciation and encouragement.

—Charles Schwab

One of the worst parts of anxiety is that it can make competent people feel insecure and start questioning their inner strengths. In our interviews, we found many high-performing people who suffer from anxiety say they constantly doubt themselves and their abilities. And yet a common problem we've found in years of executive coaching is that leaders don't express gratitude to their people about work well done—at least not anywhere nearly as frequently or effectively as they should. In fact, many leaders spend most of their time addressing performance problems, often with a focus on the below-average work of one or two team members. They assume, usually incorrectly, that those who are doing okay in their duties don't need much attention, and yet top performers can be gratitude sponges.

In interviews with thousands of employees over the past twenty years, we can attest that many feel a considerable amount of anxiety about how they're doing in their jobs. They want to know how their managers perceive the quality of their work. In fact, the highest-performing employees can often perceive lack of attention from a manager as a sign that things are not good at all. Silence can cause worry to creep up on even the best of workers.

When we advise managers to offer more positive feedback, they can push back with a litany of concerns. They say it would be nice, but they don't have the time to express more appreciation, or that their people are only interested in financial rewards. Others don't want to coddle their workers, especially during times of crisis when there are so many other demands on their time. A few leaders have shared the view that praising their people all the time for just doing their job will come across as condescending or fake. "Who am I," they ask, "a praise-giving robot?"

Well, first, it's not nonstop praise that's called for, it is *gratitude expressed in the right way and at the right time*. Managers need employees who are motivated to achieve. And one of the simplest and most effective ways to motivate people to achieve is by regularly expressing gratitude. Our research shows unequivocally that offering such positive reinforcement produces impressive boosts in team performance. Here's some of that evidence:

Research conducted for us by Willis Towers Watson found that when employee engagement is in the bottom quartile of national rankings, customer satisfaction is 20 percentage points lower than when employee engagement is in the top quartile. And of the people who report the highest level of engagement at work, a whopping 94 percent agree that their managers are effective at recognizing them when they go above and beyond. That shows an extremely strong link between gratitude and employee engagement, and engagement and customer satisfaction. All of this is made more startling when we add morale into the mix. Some 56 percent of employees who say they have low morale at work give their managers a failing grade on gratitude, while only 2 percent of people who have low morale say they have a boss who is great at appreciating their work.

How Gratitude Affects Anxiety

More than two thousand years ago, Cicero called gratitude "not only the greatest of virtues, but the parent of all others." Yet gratitude receives little attention as an area of research in the business world. That is unfortunate. Expressions of gratitude, when done regularly, can produce profound effects. In a world filled with uncertainty, when managers frequently offer up their thanks for great work—and are specific in how an achievement has helped the team—they can significantly reduce anxiety levels. Such acts are like regular deposits in the Bank of Engagement. They build up reserves for when an employee's work does have to be corrected. Workers who have a strong degree of confidence that their manager has faith in their abilities are better able to receive criticism and realize that the coaching is specific to a particular task or aspect of their work rather than a condemnation of their overall capabilities.

Another plus: Whether leaders regularly thank team members for work well done, or if they receive thanks themselves, they are better able to bounce back from adversity with greater resilience, according to Dr. Sara Algoe, associate professor at the University of North Carolina at Chapel Hill. Her research has found a substantial link between gratitude and employee efficiency and productivity. "Gratitude is important for forming and maintaining the most important relationships of our lives, those with the people we interact with every day," she says. Her work shows employees who express and receive gratitude at work are also more likely to volunteer for tasks, step up to accomplish hard things, and work better as a part of a team. Furthermore, her research shows that leaders who regularly offer gratitude are scored higher by their team members on measured attributes of compassion, consideration, empathy, and (gasp) even love.

We aren't talking here about general praise that has little meaning, e.g., "Good work, team." We like to remind leaders that if you can say it to a dog, it's not gratitude. No, what we are talking about is gratitude offered to another person with sincerity and specificity for what they've contributed. When anyone accepts such thanks, neurotransmitters in the brain release dopamine and serotonin, which are responsible for a good mood. By consciously practicing gratitude, we can strengthen these neural pathways and create a physiological superhighway to harmony within our team members.

Chris Schembra, author of *Gratitude and Pasta*, has hosted hundreds of gratitude intervention dinners in New York City, where companies can better engage with their clients or employees. At each of the 7:47 Club dinners (the time the meal starts), Chris asks his guests the same question: "If you could give credit and thanks to one person in your life, who you don't give enough credit or thanks to, who would that be?"

Schembra told us, "People often walk into our dinners feeling lonely, unfulfilled, disconnected, insecure. They listen to others share the stories from their past about their mothers, fathers, dogs, third-grade teachers, ex-girlfriends. They realize they're not as alone as they thought. Everybody can relate to a mother, whether she deserted them or nurtured them; a grandpa who took them to soccer practice. By sharing our histories we decrease anxiety."

The 7:47 Club's research director Madeline Haslam points to the vital role of leaders in setting an example with gratitude. In 1961, Albert Bandura at Stanford University conducted what has become known as the Bobo doll experiment. The professor filmed adults behaving aggressively toward a Bobo doll, an inflatable clown that bounces back up after being pushed or punched. A test group of children later watched the videos and were placed in a room with the doll; other children watched no video. "If the children saw adults beating up the doll, they displayed much more physical aggression to the doll than the control group," said Haslam. "This observational learning does not just happen with children. If you observe a leader practice gratitude to others in front of you, it teaches you to do it. It inspires employees with the emotion to go forward and follow that example."

How Gratitude Helps Us Handle Pressure

Another bit of good news for managers: Gratitude helps people develop a greater capacity to handle stress. Studies by a team of scientists led by Rollin McCraty, psycho-physiologist and professor at Florida Atlantic University, show that those who give or receive gratitude have a marked reduction in their level of cortisol, the stress hormone. They also are more resilient to emotional setbacks and negative experiences. McCraty's work suggests humans can rewire their brains to deal with tough circumstances with more awareness and broader perception, merely by acknowledging and appreciating the little steps forward in their lives.

This is especially important because anxiety can make talented people feel like frauds, their external validation not matching up with what they feel internally. That's called the imposter syndrome—waiting for the world to find out we aren't all we are cracked up to be. In the ranks of celebrities, this is more common than we might imagine.

Rock star Bruce Springsteen's autobiography *Born to Run* outlines his lifelong battle with self-doubt and feeling like a "complete fake." Comedian Steve Martin, in his autobiography *Born Standing Up*, details his two-decades-long struggle with bouts of anxiety and full-blown panic attacks. Lady Gaga, who appears to be the epitome of confidence with her assortment of outrageous outfits and amazing live performances, has openly discussed her anxiety. On an HBO special, she said, "I still sometimes feel like a loser kid in high school, and I just have to pick myself up and tell myself that I'm a superstar every morning so that I can get through this day and be for my fans what they need for me to be."

Eventually, without support and coping mechanisms, even talented people can burn out from stress and anxiety. UCLA neuroscientist Dr. Alex Korb explains that a person who worries over and over about unfavorable outcomes will wire his brain to focus on nothing but the negative. He argues that our minds cannot focus on positive and negative information simultaneously. By consciously practicing gratitude in a team, he says, we could help train our brains to selectively attend to positive emotions and thoughts. This can reduce anxiety and feelings of apprehension.

People tend to focus more on the challenges of life, because challenges demand action. And at work, isn't it our job to overcome challenges? We tend to pay scant attention to the good things because we feel that we don't have to do much to make them stick around. And yet gratitude helps people focus on the positives, fight negative thoughts with optimism, accept harsh realities, and let others know they are cared for and appreciated.

One of the most effective ways leaders can combat anxiety is to foster an attitude of gratitude throughout their organizations—not just top-down, but peer-to-peer. We were visiting a hospital one Friday and were privileged to witness a special meeting. Each week one staff member received what they called the Grace Under Fire trophy, a fire hose mounted on a block of wood. The award was brought out to much applause, and was given from peer-to-peer as a way to recognize something admirable that a staff member had done during the week. In the case we watched, a nurse had nominated a fellow staff member who had taken one of her weekend shifts. The scheduled eight hours had turned into twelve as the ER filled up, but the substitute kept her cool. In presenting the award, the nominating nurse not only expressed her deep appreciation, but spoke about core values like dependability and teamwork.

The team's manager later told us that this Friday ritual has not only added a touch of fun but has elevated everyone's behavior and strengthened relationships. The award presentation was fast (followed by well-deserved snacks), and yet it reinforced in a powerful way what the staff members valued the most: keeping cool under pressure while helping each other.

Turn Doubts into Assurance

As we have visited worksites like this and talked with leaders throughout the world, we have found some other practical methods whereby gratitude can turn doubts into assurance.

Method 1: Make Gratitude Clear, Specific, and Sincere

Generic comments around the workplace such as "great work" have never cut it, especially when it comes to reassuring anxious team members. Employees hear such nonspecific praise and tend to dismiss it, especially those who may be feeling self-doubt. Instead, grateful leaders home in on a particular aspect of an achievement or manner in which a person is going about their work. For instance, "Nice job on that report" is good, and certainly better than saying nothing. But better yet would be to say something to the effect of "I love how your report provides a short narrative to go along with the numbers. That overview of the market and our place in it was very helpful when we had to explain the findings to the executive team. Nice job."

Carlos Aguilera, director of Avis Budget Group's premium brand strategy, is one of the best managers we've seen at making gratitude specific to the company's values. When we met him, he was general manager of the Dallas Fort Worth Airport location, and his team's pre-shift meetings would always kick off with specific gratitude. He'd ask: "Okay, who saw someone doing something great yesterday?" One day we were with Aguilera when a shift supervisor suggested Delana should be singled out. She had noticed one of her customers wearing a knee brace and, without being asked, called an attendant in the back and asked for the customer's rental car to be brought up front so the person wouldn't have to walk through the lot. The story took only thirty seconds to tell, and we noted the energy in the pre-shift huddle starting to build. Best of all, Delana knew that her managers were paying attention and grateful of her attention to detail.

Aguilera presented her with an on-the-spot award. "And we make sure each accomplishment is posted on the bulletin board," Aguilera told us later. It was the little things like this that kept his people energized. He was trusted, communicated well, and spent an inordinate amount of time with his high-potential people. When we studied Aguilera, he had the highest employee engagement scores in the entire twenty-six-thousand-person company. And what he learned to do can be replicated.

Method 2: Match Gratitude to Magnitude

We certainly encourage managers to recognize small accomplishments on a regular basis. But when a team member does something big, leaders need to make sure gratitude is commensurate with the accomplishment. When a reward for an achievement is not aligned with the impact, it might do more harm than good.

"In the past, one department had implemented a program where they gave a ten-dollar gift certificate to recognize extra effort and say thank you," said Shari Rife, manager of creative process and facilitation for Rich Products Corporation, a $4 billion food company in Buffalo, New York. It didn't matter what action was being recognized; the recognition remained the same.

"It was very informal, without much criteria surrounding it," she told us. "And it caused real frustration with associates because someone who cleaned out the supply cabinet was recognized in the same way as someone who implemented a huge project. Because they both got the same gift card, it actually became de-motivating."

When leaders align rewards with the level of achievement, they help those who are anxious make more positive assumptions about their work. For small steps forward, verbal praise or a note of thanks is appropriate, but bigger achievements require a tangible reward presented in a timely manner. These include actions that bring a financial benefit to the organization, save or win a big client, improve a major process, or make the organization better in a substantial way.

Method 3: Preserve Gratitude's Significance

An employee we interviewed said, "My boss said I was going to be recognized in front of our team for reaching one year of service. The company did these service awards all the time, and they were nice things, so I said that'd be okay." But when the big day arrived, the employee found out they were going to tack his award presentation on after another—a woman who was receiving a twenty-year service award. "All these people from outside our department showed up and it was like a eulogy," he said. "Folks were crying and telling her how much they loved her. I wanted to crawl into a hole. I hardly knew anyone yet. When they got around to my turn, the people who had come from other departments couldn't just up and walk away, so they stayed and watched my miserable little one-year award being given. A couple of my team members said nice things, but compared to the lovefest we'd all just witnessed it was embarrassing."

He darkly joked that it was like giving out the Sound Mixing Oscar *after* the award for Best Picture. He added, "Later, when my manager told me we'd be celebrating my three-year anniversary—that was the next one they gave out an award for—I told him they could do it without me. There was no way in hell I was going to be there."

The point: Whenever you express gratitude, do not dampen the result by combining it with other business. Also, do not minimize accomplishments. If you talk about lessons learned (*Rebecca sure has come a long way*) or if you try to socialize the experience (*Good work, Trey. I wish I could recognize everyone on our team*), you will most likely diminish the positive effect your gratitude would otherwise have provided.

The last warning is to acknowledge the difference between recognition and celebration. Some managers are reticent to single out individuals. Instead of recognizing the above-and-beyond contributions of one or two people in each staff meeting, say, they'll take the whole team to lunch once a month. That's not recognition, it's a celebration. And it may create more anxiety for high achievers, who often are eager to know

their work is valued. Individual recognition and team cele-
brations serve unique but different roles in building a high-
performing team.

Method 4: Provide Gratitude to High-Flyers, Too

As leaders spread gratitude around their teams, it's common
for them to realize that there's great value in not only rewarding big wins, but regularly praising achievements that meet
expectations. We believe Chloe, who we introduced in Chapter 1, needed this kind of reinforcement that her work was
valued. Yet some managers take this socialism of gratitude
to extremes and begin to worry that everyone is treated fairly
and that no one gets hurt feelings.

While giving everyone a chance to shine is important—and
leaders need to ensure that all team members are acknowledged
for their unique achievements on a regular basis—it's also
vital not to hold back with high achievers. Offering appreciation is not just about strengthening those that may lack
confidence, it's also about reinforcing the work of those who
seem to have plenty of confidence, those who are constantly
going above and beyond.

In many cases, managers don't want to be seen as playing
favorites or fawning over their "stars." The leader of an engineering design team told us he learned a lesson about this
the hard way. Jennifer, he said, was "by far my most innovative and productive designer." The problem was, he didn't
want to give Jennifer too much praise because she was *always*
so good. "Frankly, Jeff worked right next to Jennifer, and I

didn't want him to feel bad." The manager also knew Jennifer was confident in her abilities and decided she probably didn't need that many pats on the back. But it turned out that she, like most people, wanted to know her work was truly appreciated. "Over time I think Jennifer felt undervalued," the manager said, reporting that "she left for a competitor a while ago." When we asked if Jeff was still there, the manager chuckled sadly. Of course. Jeff wasn't going anywhere.

The bottom line: Gratitude is an anxiety reliever; and it can serve as the oxygen in the room that fuels engagement for all team members—especially for high achievers who are often gratitude sponges.

Method 5: Keep Gratitude Close to the Action

To help quell anxious feelings, gratitude should occur soon after an achievement. When team members do something above and beyond and then hear nothing from their manager for days or weeks, they can start to worry. To be recognized later is of some consequence, but frankly, in 99 percent of cases, when managers put it off, they forget. If leaders want to reinforce the right behaviors, they should keep gratitude close to the action—soon after they see good things happening.

Gratitude also must be frequent. Those who feel heightened anxiety generally require a steady flow of reassurance that their work is adding value, and when times are tough that need increases. Our research finds that in the best teams, highly engaged employees feel praised for their specific accomplishments on a regular basis—at least once a week.

"In the most innovative companies, there is a significantly higher volume of thank-yous than in companies of low innovation," says Professor Rosabeth Moss Kanter of Harvard. With our research, we've been thrilled to find higher levels of gratitude not only in the innovative workplaces we studied, but in cultures of great customer service, operational excellence, compassion, and ownership. In the best cultures, teammates have each other's backs, and they spend much more time thanking each other peer-to-peer. These seemingly warm and fuzzy skills create tangible esprit de corps and a single-mindedness about living the right behaviors.

It is through timely reinforcement that people grow to their full stature. To know they are on the right path, workers need frequent, specific gratitude.

Build Confidence with Gratitude

- One of the simplest and most effective ways to motivate employees to achieve is by regularly expressing gratitude. Research shows offering positive reinforcement produces impressive boosts in team performance and significantly reduces anxiety levels in team members.

- Leaders don't express gratitude to their people about work well done anywhere nearly as frequently or effectively as they should.

- High-performing employees are often gratitude sponges and perceive a lack of attention from a manager as a sign that things are not good; silence can cause worry to creep up on even the best of workers.

- Regular expressions of gratitude are like deposits in a Bank of Engagement. They build up reserves for when an employee's work has to be corrected. Research shows gratitude also helps people develop a greater capacity to handle stress.

- Other practical methods to turn doubts into assurance include: 1) make gratitude clear, specific, and sincere, 2) match gratitude to magnitude, 3) preserve gratitude's significance, 4) provide gratitude to high-flyers, too, and 5) keep gratitude close to the action.

SUMMARY

Conclusion
THE SEMICOLON:
BEFORE AND AFTER

There are moments which mark your life . . . when you realize
nothing will ever be the same and time is divided into two parts:
before this, and after this.

—Denzel Washington (as John Hobbes)

While a first step in building a healthy work culture comes
in the form of awareness—of acknowledging the frantic
duck-paddling going on under the surface in your team—the
second part, mitigation, comes when we begin to minimize
anxiety, offer support for people to work through their feelings, and build resilience for challenges to come. Sometimes
it's as simple as being accepting.

Take the example of Madalyn Parker, who, when we became aware of her story, worked for Olark, a Michigan-based
software company. Parker is a talented software developer
and explained that she suffers from chronic anxiety, depression, and post-traumatic stress disorder. Every now and then
she needs to take some time to focus on her well-being.

After several nights of insomnia, Parker had sent an email
to her team saying she'd be out of the office for a few days

to focus on her mental health. The next day, she opened her inbox to find a flood of supportive missives. One that caught her eye was from company CEO Ben Congleton. "I can't believe this is not a standard practice at all organizations," read part of his email. "You are an example to us all . . . and help cut through the stigma so we can all bring our whole selves to work."

Said Parker, "I was absolutely touched. It brought tears to my eyes. It was surprising to be applauded for my vulnerability."

Strong, caring leaders like Congleton can do a lot to help, making a huge difference for not only those who suffer but everyone on their teams. More leaders are beginning to understand the issues surrounding mental health and are truly caring about their employees' well-being. They are creating work environments where goals such as "happy" and "healthy" are taken just as seriously as sales quotas or customer satisfaction. Derek Lundsten, president and CEO of LifeGuides, told us, "It's time to build a bridge between the old model where employees left their problems at the door and a new world where we set time and space aside for those conversations to take place."

We aren't there yet. It will take a new way of thinking; maybe even a new way of punctuating.

Heather Parrie, a Missouri accountant, is the type of person whose accomplishments used to fill up her Facebook page. A few years ago, she was hit with something unexpected. Burdened with the weight of expectations and relentlessly comparing herself to successful friends, she began to crumble. In the grips of self-doubt, anxiety, and depression, she started sleeping up to twenty hours a day. She canceled plans with friends, skipped work, and preferred to stay wrapped in a safe cocoon of blankets. She ended up being let go from her job, which just made things worse. Even in her darkest moments, when she felt she'd never get out of bed, Parrie managed to conceal her inner battle from friends and family.

After battling alone for many months, she began finding help with therapy, medication, and opening up to those she loves. She described her reasons for getting a tattoo of a semicolon. In literary terms, a semicolon is used when an author could've chosen to end their sentence but chose not to. It is used to pause—to take a breath—but another phrase always follows, one that can stand alone and independent of the first. For Parrie, and many more, that punctuation mark has become a symbol of the fight to continue writing their story with anxiety or any other mental health issue. She talks about a daily struggle to overcome the duality of her carefully crafted outward appearance of success versus her inward battle against perceived failure.

Today, the semicolon has become one of the most popular tattoos in ink shops from Peoria to Paris. It symbolizes the concept of "before and after." For those who suffer from anxiety overload, and for those leaders who watch over teams of human beings, the semicolon might symbolize a next step in all our progression. We aren't suggesting any of us run to the closest ink shop and roll up our sleeves, but we are hoping that we all consider what entrenched behaviors we might be holding on to as leaders that are negatively affecting us, and those around us; then, we should take a breath and consider a new path using a few of the ideas we've shared in this book.

In the world *before*, discussing subjects like anxiety was taboo, including and accommodating those who didn't fit the mold too much work, biases and judgment all too common. In the world *after*, individualism will be valued; needless, harmful anxiety lessened; and those who struggle accepted with compassion.

We hope you agree that it's time to punctuate.

Acknowledgments

We thank our agent Jim Levine, who grasped how important this topic could be and supported us from day one. Similarly, we were touched by the enthusiasm for the work of our editors Hollis Heimbouch and Rebecca Raskin of Harper Business.

We owe a debt of gratitude to our critical reader Emily Loose, and we thank Christy Lawrence, who arranged many of the interviews and spent countless hours transcribing. Appreciation goes to our team at FindMojo.com: Paul Yoachum, Lance Garvin, Brianna Bateman, Bryce Morgan, Tanner Smith, Asher Gunsay, Garrett Elton, Mark Durham, and Jaren Durham.

We thank Mark Fortier and Norbert Beatty, our publicists, and Brian Perrin and his team at Harper Business marketing. And we appreciate all those who are quoted herein; we were enriched by your wisdom.

Finally, we are so thankful to our families for their support: to Jennifer, who has kept this project moving with her enthusiasm and profound insights. And to Heidi and to Cassi and Braeden; Carter, Luisa, Lucas Chester, and Clara Iris; Brinden; and Garrett and Maile.

Notes

Sources quoted in *Anxiety at Work* are from firsthand interviews with the authors unless noted below.

Chapter 1: The Duck Syndrome

3 In a 2018 survey, 34 percent of workers: The citation is from an American Psychological Association survey of 3,458 adults, quoted in the *Wall Street Journal*, "The Most Anxious Generation Goes to Work," by Sue Shellenbarger, May 9, 2019. The statistic indicating 18 percent of adults have an anxiety disorder is from the Anxiety and Depression Association of America website "Facts & Statistics" backed up by the American Psychiatric Association statistics on its Center for Workplace Mental Health website and the article "Anxiety Disorders: Why They Matter and What Employers Can Do."

3 Harvard Medical School research claimed: The research and quote are from the Harvard Health Publishing article "Mental Health Problems in the Workplace," February 2010.

4 workplace anxiety is estimated to cost some $40 billion: The $40 billion statistic is found in the Health.com article "How to Relieve the Acute Discomfort of Anxiety Disorders," posted on February 29, 2016; the $300 billion statistic is in the Healthline article "Stress Costs U.S. $300 Billion Every Year," by Gillian Mohney, January 15, 2018; and the 600 billion euros statistic in Europe is from the Euroactiv.com article "Mental Health Issues Cost EU Countries More Than €600 Billion," by Beatriz Rios, November 29, 2018.

4 According to a 2019 study published in the *Harvard Business Review*: The data on young people leaving jobs for mental health reasons comes from CNBC, "Half of Millennials and 75% of Gen-Zers Have Left Jobs for Mental Health Reasons," by Cory Stieg, October 8, 2019.

5 says Michael Fenlon, chief people officer for PricewaterhouseCoopers: Michael Fenlon is summarized from the *Wall Street Journal* article "The Most Anxious Generation Goes to Work," by Sue Shellenbarger, May 9, 2019.

5 90 percent judged it would be a bad idea to confide their situation: The statistic is from the theladders.com article "The Surprising Group Has the Most Workplace Anxiety," by C. W. Headley, posted on December 2, 2019, quoting a study by ZenBusiness.

6 According to the U.S. Census Bureau, by May 2020: The Census Bureau data (from a survey conducted with the Centers for Disease Control) finding 30 percent of Americans show signs of clinical anxiety is from the *Washington Post* article "A Third of Americans Now Show Signs of Clinical Anxiety or Depression,

Census Bureau Finds amid Coronavirus Pandemic," by Alyssa Fowers and William Wan, May 26, 2020.

11 Only one in four people who suffer from anxiety: That only one in four people with anxiety have spoken with their bosses is from the humanagehr.com article "Why Aren't We Talking More about Mental Health in the Workplace?," posted on May 17, 2020.

11 The term "the duck syndrome" was coined at Stanford University: Covered in the *Stanford Daily* article "Duck Syndrome and a Culture of Misery," by Tiger Sun, January 31, 2018.

11 A *USA Today* poll of organizations found up to half: The *USA Today* findings on ghosting were in the article "Workers Are 'Ghosting' Interviews, Blowing off Work in a Strong Job Market," by Paul Davidson, July 19, 2018.

13 workplace stress and anxiety may be a contributing factor: Research linking workplace stress and anxiety to 120,000 deaths annually is from the Graduate School of Stanford Business website article "Why Your Workplace Might Be Killing You," by Shana Lynch, posted on February 23, 2015, quoting research from Professor Jeffrey Pfeffer et al.

15 One study found 86 percent of those with high anxiety: The data linking anxiety and productivity is from a study of 1,004 people with anxiety found in the ZenBusiness.com article "Anxiety in the Workplace," November 20, 2019.

15 Mensa members have been found to suffer from anxiety disorders: The study on Mensa members was noted in the *Scientific American* article "Bad News for the Highly Intelligent," by David Hambrick, December 5, 2017.

15 Take the recent transformation of the England men's national football (soccer) team: Information was taken from the *HRDirector* article "Leadership Lessons from Gareth Southgate's Team Transformation," by Jeremy Snape, July 11, 2018; the *Guardian* article "How the Psychology of the England Football Team Could Change Your Life," by Emine Saner, July 10, 2018; and the BusinessLeader.com article "Seven Leadership Lessons Learned from Gareth Southgate," by Barney Cotton, July 9, 2018.

17 by the famous primatologist Dian Fossey: Dr. Dian Fossey's account of anxious apes is from Sarah Wilson's *First, We Make the Beast Beautiful*, Dey Street Books (2018).

18 The concept is so important to the U.S. Army: Information on the U.S. Army's resilience training is from the PositivePsychology.com article "Resilience Training: How to Master Mental Toughness and Thrive," by Dr. Catherine Moore, April 9, 2020; more in this section was gleaned from the *Psychology Today* article "Why Some People Are More Resilient than Others," by Denise Cummings, March 11, 2015.

19 as renowned University of Pennsylvania psychologist: Dr. Martin Seligman wrote about his theory of teaching resilience in the *Harvard Business Review*, April 2011 edition, in the aptly titled article "Building Resilience."

20 PricewaterhouseCoopers has found: PWC's data on return on equity for mental health investments by companies is from the company's white paper "Creating a Mentally Healthy Workplace: Return on Investment Analysis," March 2014.

20 *Forbes* reports the total cost of overall poor employee health: From the *Forbes* article "Poor Worker Health Costs U.S. Employers Half Trillion Dollars a Year," by Bruce Japsen, November 15, 2018.

21 Harvard Medical School research adds: Quote is from the Harvard Health Publishing article "Mental Health Problems in the Workplace," February 2010.

28 According to management consulting firm McKinsey: Quote is from the McKinsey.com article "Tuning In, Turning Outward: Cultivating Compassionate Leadership in a Crisis," by Nicolai Chen Nielsen, Gemma D'Auria, and Sasha Zolley, May 1, 2020.

Chapter 2: How Anxiety Fills the Gap

31 By July 2020, 60 percent of American workers: The data about Americans concerned with job security comes from a Wavemaker survey reported on MediaPost.com in the article "Wavemaker Study Finds Americans Worry about Job Security, Economy," by Larissa Faw, July 10, 2020.

32 In his book *Kids These Days*: *Kids These Days* was written by Malcolm Harris and published by Little, Brown & Company (2017). We quote Harris from the *Vox* article "Why Are Millennials Burned Out? Capitalism," by Sean Illing, March 16, 2019.

33 Sam Cassell was a terrific free-throw shooter: Cassell's clutch free-throw shooting record is outlined on 82games.com in the article "Random Stat: Clutch Free-Throw Shooting," where you may be able to determine the identity of the mystery player who didn't do as well under pressure.

34 In the *Atlantic*, Ashley Fetters: Fetters's comments are summarized from her *Atlantic* article "College Is Different for the School-Shooting Generation," November 11, 2018; and the *Akron Beacon Journal* article "Megan McArdle: How Did We End up Raising Generation Paranoia?," by Megan McArdle, November 17, 2018.

35 Four times as many millennials as Gen Xers list: The data that four times as many millennials as Gen Xers list "fear of losing job" as a top concern is from the *Forbes* article "Millennial Anxiety in the Workplace," by Clara Knutson, July 31, 2012.

37 One need look no further than the decline of Yahoo: The account is from the *New York Times* article "Yahoo's Brain Drain Shows a Loss of Faith Inside the Company," by Vindu Goel, January 10, 2016; and the *New York Post* article "No Layoffs . . . This Week: Marissa Mayer's Creepy Comment Kills Morale," by James Covert and Claire Atkinson, January 18, 2016.

39 Take General Electric as another unfortunate case: GE's tough times were noted in the *Wall Street Journal* article "How Jeffrey Immelt's 'Success Theater' Masked the Rot at GE," by Thomas Gryta, Joann S. Lublin, and David Benoit, February 21, 2018.

39 Six months into the job, we were heartened: Larry Culp was quoted from his appearance on *Mad Money* on CNBC in the CNBC article "GE Will Be Transparent about Challenges in Its Turnaround Plan, CEO Larry Culp says," by Tyler Clifford, March 14, 2019.

40 by 2013, executives at AT&T: The account of AT&T was chronicled from the *Harvard Business Review* article "AT&T's Talent Overhaul," by John Donovan and Cathy Benko, October 2016.

44 Evidence on the value of frequent check-ins: The BetterWorks data was quoted from the *Fast Company* article "Why the Annual Performance Review Is Going Extinct," by Kris Duggan, October 20, 2015.

44 According to a Leadership IQ survey of thirty thousand people: The survey is quoted from the *Forbes* article "Fewer Than Half of Employees Know if They're Doing a Good Job," by Mark Murphy, September 4, 2016.

50 When Lutz Ziob was general manager of Microsoft Learning: Lutz Ziob's story was told to us by Liz Wiseman and confirmed by Ziob.

51 more than half of workers say their managers become more closed-minded: That more than half of managers become more controlling during crisis is from the *Harvard Business Review* article "When Managers Break Down Under Pressure, So Do Their Teams," by David Maxfield and Justin Hale, December 17, 2018.

57 This is such an important concept that "Bias for Action": Amazon's principle of "Bias for Action" was found on aboutamazon.com under "Our Leadership Principles."

59 according to *Forbes*, nine out of ten managers: The statistic that managers shy away from giving feedback is from the *Forbes* article "Today's Workers Are Hungry for Feedback; Here's How to Give It to Them," by G. Riley Mills, September 27, 2019.

59 65 percent of today's workers feel shortchanged: The statistic that employees want more feedback is from the *Forbes* article "65% of Employees Want More Feedback (So Why Don't They Get It?)," by Victor Lipman, August 8, 2016.

65 A leader who was effective at this kind of upward communication: James Rogers's story was taken from the *Harvard Business Review* article "Leadership Is a Conversation," by Boris Groysberg and Michael Slind, June 2012.

Chapter 3: How to Turn Less into More

69 Brandon Webb passed the challenge: Webb is quoted, and information gleaned on the Navy SEALs, from the Observer.com article "Bulletproof Mind: 6 Secrets of Mental Toughness from the Navy SEALs," by Charles Chu, November 25, 2016, and from interviews with Dr. Rita McGrath.

71 global staffing firm Robert Half showed: The 91 percent statistic on burnout is from the *Inc.* article "In a New Study, 90 Percent of Employees Admit to Feeling Burned Out. Here Are 3 Ways to Successfully Manage It," by Michael Schneider, September 24, 2019.

71 As Adam Grant of the Wharton School: Dr. Grant is quoted from his *New York Times* article "Burnout Isn't Just in Your Head. It's in Your Circumstances," March 19, 2020.

72 Adrienne Boissy, MD, chief experience officer: Dr. Boissy is quoted from her article on the Cleveland Clinic website "Why Resilience Training Isn't the Antidote for Burnout," posted on October 2, 2017.

74 Employees who report being burned out: Gallup's data on burnout, sick leave, and turnover is from the Gallup.com article "Employee Burnout, Part 1: The 5 Main Causes," by Ben Wigert and Sangeeta Agrawal, July 12, 2018.

74 burned-out employees account for: The $190 billion number from Bain & Company is from the *Harvard Business Review* article "Employee Burnout Is a Problem with the Company, Not the Person," by Eric Garton, April 6, 2017.

75 Harvard psychologist Harry Levinson: Dr. Levinson is quoted from his *Harvard Business Review* article "When Executives Burn Out," July–August 1996.

78 in 1939, Kurt Lewin conducted: There are numerous accounts of Lewin's work in the Harwood factory; we especially appreciated the *Journal of Applied*

Behavioral Science article "Kurt Lewin and the Harwood Studies: The Foundations of OD," by Dr. Bernard Burnes, June 2007.

79 As Adam Goodman: Dr. Goodman is quoted from the *Fast Company* article "How Managers Can Help Employees Avoid Burnout," by Stephanie Vozza, October 5, 2018.

80 "It's important to make sure your employees understand": Liane Davey and Kyle Arteaga are quoted from the *Harvard Business Review* article "Make Sure Your Team's Workload Is Divided Fairly," by Rebecca Knight, November 14, 2016.

83 counseled Harvard's Harry Levinson: Dr. Levinson is again quoted from his *Harvard Business Review* article "When Executives Burn Out," July–August 1996.

83 A study among nurses in the United States: The study was found in the National Library of Medicine article "Effects of Job Rotation and Role Stress among Nurses on Job Satisfaction and Organizational Commitment," by Dr. Wen-Hsien Ho, January 12, 2009, and published by BMC Health Services Research, February 2009.

84 A practitioner of job rotating is Matthew Ross: Ross is quoted from the *Forbes* article "6 Unconventional Yet Effective Ways to Boost Motivation and Inspire a High-Performance Culture," by Heidi Lynne Kurter, April 23, 2019.

85 As Jamie Dimon, CEO of JPMorgan Chase: Dimon is quoted from Patricia Crisafulli's *The House of Dimon*, Wiley (2011).

85 Shelly Lazarus, chairman emeritus of Ogilvy & Mather: Shelly Lazarus was first interviewed and quoted in Adrian Gostick and Dana Telford's *The Integrity Advantage*, Gibbs Smith (2003).

87 employees who have a manager who's willing to listen: Gallup's 62 percent number is from the HRAsiaMedia.com article "Bosses Need to Be Proactive to Prevent Employee Burnout," February 7, 2020.

89 In a series of experiments conducted by PhDs Joshua Rubinstein: Dr. Rubinstein's research is encapsulated on the American Psychological Association website in the article "Multitasking: Switching Costs," posted on March 20, 2006.

90 A University of London study shows: The study was reported on in the *Sydney Morning Herald* article "The Multi-tasking Myth," April 15, 2013.

90 In the biography *Abraham Lincoln*: Carl Sandburg wrote about Lincoln in *Abraham Lincoln: The Prairie Years & The War Years*, Harcourt Brace & World (1939).

91 how one manager was helping reduce distractions: We introduced Kim Cochran to readers in Adrian Gostick and Chester Elton's *The Best Team Wins*, Simon & Schuster (2018).

Chapter 4: Clear Paths Forward

98 While 40 percent of boomers stayed: Baby boomer longevity with an employer was from the *PBS News Hour* story "Poll Reveals Age, Income Influence People's Loyalty to an Employer," May 11, 2016.

98 78 percent of Gen Zers and 43 percent of millennials surveyed: Statistics on Gen Zers and millennials planning to leave their jobs within two years is from the Society for Human Resources Management website article "Generation Z and Millennials Seek Recognition at Work," by Stephen Miller, September 12, 2019.

98 According to Brookings Institution data: The data is from the Brookings .edu article "Low-Wage Work Is More Pervasive Than You Think, and There Aren't

Enough 'Good Jobs' to Go Around," by Martha Ross and Nicole Bateman, November 21, 2019.

99 according to a 2018 study by ManPowerGroup: The study was reported on in the *Inc.* article "Here's the Number 1 Criteria the Largest Generation in the Workforce Looks for in Employers," by Adam Robinson, September 7, 2018.

99 A Gallup poll of millennials: Gallup's data on 87 percent of millennials valuing growth is from the Gallup.com article "Millennials Want Jobs to Be Development Opportunities," by Amy Adkins and Brandon Rigoni, June 30, 2016.

100 Research by Deloitte has found: Deloitte's data on organizations that nurture a desire to learn are market leaders is from the *Harvard Business Review* article "4 Ways to Create a Learning Culture on Your Team," by Thomas Chamorro-Premuzic and Josh Bersin, July 12, 2018.

100 We agree with J. Maureen Henderson: Henderson is quoted from her *Forbes* article "Job Stability vs. Job Satisfaction? Millennials May Have to Settle for Neither," December 22, 2012.

100 According to Corporate Executive Board research: The data on learning cultures is also from the *Harvard Business Review* article "4 Ways to Create a Learning Culture on Your Team," by Thomas Chamorro-Premuzic and Josh Bersin, July 12, 2018.

101 More than 75 percent of Gen Z workers: This data is from the *Business Insider* article "Gen Z Workers Expect a Promotion after One Year on the Job, and Their Bosses Are Creating New Titles and Throwing 'Workversary' Parties to Keep Them Happy," by Allana Akhtar, April 9, 2019.

101 The company's founder and CEO: Marc Cenedella is quoted from his TheLadders.com article "This Is How I Got Millennials to Stop Asking about Promotions," July 21, 2017.

116 little alignment to their day-to-day needs: Drs. Steve Glaveski and Matthieu Boisgontier are quoted from the *Harvard Business Review* article "Where Companies Go Wrong with Learning and Development," by Steve Glaveski, October 2, 2019.

117 This point was stressed to us by Dan Helfrich: Helfrich was introduced to our readers in *The Best Team Wins*, Simon & Schuster (2018).

118 we advise taking the approach recommended: Dr. Sydney Finkelstein is quoted from his *Harvard Business Review* article "Why a One-Size-Fits-All Approach to Employee Development Doesn't Work," March 5, 2019.

120 Margaret Rogers, vice president of Pariveda Solutions: Rogers is quoted from her *Harvard Business Review* article "A Better Way to Develop and Retain Top Talent," January 20, 2020.

122 Dr. LaMesha Craft of National Intelligence University: Dr. Craft is quoted from her govloop.com article "Peer-to-Peer Learning, the Most Powerful Tool in the Workplace," March 12, 2018.

122 In their book *The Expertise Economy*: Palmer and Blake are quoted from *The Expertise Economy*, Nicholas Brealey (2018).

Chapter 5: How "It's Not Perfect" Can Become "It's Good, I'll Move On"

125 mocked by cultural satirists *The Simpsons*: The dialogue is quoted from season 3, episode 12 of *The Simpsons*, "I Married Marge" (1991).

127 In the 1940s and '50s, Callas: We cite the *Washington Post* article "Callas:

Opera's Human Voice," by Tim Page, September 24, 1995. We also note the work of Amii Barnard-Bahn and her April 17, 2020, YouTube post, "How Perfection Can Hinder Your Leadership: What Can You Learn from an Opera Diva"; and the SlippedDisk.com article "Exclusive: My Life with Maria Callas," by Norman Lebrecht, posted on May 31, 2016.

128 In recapping her career: Callas's quote about courage was told to Peter Dragadze and recounted in Nicholas Petsalès-Diomèdès's *The Unknown Callas: The Greek Years*, Amadeus (2001).

128 Perfectionists aren't merely ambitious: The quote from Dr. Brian Swider is from the *Harvard Business Review* article "The Pros and Cons of Perfectionism, According to Research," by Drs. Brian Swider, Dana Harari, Amy P. Breidenthal, and Laurens Bujold Steed, December 27, 2018.

129 Benjamin Cherkasky, a therapist and researcher: Cherkasky is quoted from the *Chicago Tribune* article "The Overachieving Generation: As Millennials Strive for Perfection, Anxiety and Depression Increase," by Alison Bowen, October 31, 2018.

130 In a 2017 study: Dr. Thomas Curran's work is from the *Harvard Business Review* article "Perfectionism Is Increasing, and That's Not Good News," by Thomas Curran and Andrew P. Hill, January 26, 2018.

132 The work of Paul Hewitt: Drs. Hewitt and Flett's work was captured in the *Vox* article "Perfectionism Is Killing Us," by Christie Aschwanden, December 5, 2019.

133 In terms of spotting that someone is a perfectionist: Dr. Alice Boyes's work is best found in her book *The Anxiety Toolkit*, Tarcher Perigee (2015).

133 Harvard University research adds: This information on perfectionists versus healthy strivers is from the paper "Perfectionism: Strategies for Change," by Dr. Jennifer Page Hughes, 2013 (revised 2014), issued by the Center for Academic and Personal Development, Harvard University.

136 According to new research from Forrester Consulting: The research is from the *Harvard Business Review* article "How Companies Can Learn to Make Faster Decisions," by Eric Winquist, September 29, 2014.

137 Stanford psychologist Carol Dweck: Dr. Dweck's work can be found in *Mindset*, Ballantine Books (2007).

142 A great example of creating a system: SpaceX's example is also from the *Harvard Business Review* article "How Companies Can Learn to Make Faster Decisions," by Eric Winquist, September 29, 2014.

Chapter 6: From Conflict Avoidance to Healthy Debate

157 We admire the thinking of Drs. Emma Seppälä: Drs. Seppälä and Cameron's work is found in the *Harvard Business Review* article "Proof That Positive Work Cultures Are More Productive," by Emma Seppälä and Kim Cameron, December 1, 2015.

160 Linda Gravett, a Cincinnati-based psychologist: Dr. Gravett is quoted from the *Chicago Tribune* article "Millennials Struggle with Confrontation at Work," by Rex Huppke, November 19, 2012.

160 Deb Muller, CEO of HR Acuity: Muller is quoted from her HRAcuity .com article "Are Millennials More Conflict-Averse Than Other Generations?," posted on September 25, 2017.

163 "Although deferring a difficult conversation": Amy Jen Su was quoted from her *Harvard Business Review* article "Giving Feedback When You're Conflict Averse," August 13, 2015.

163 "By naming names": We quote from Drs. Porter-O'Grady and Malloch's *Quantum Leadership*, Stanford Business Books (2019).

165 a terrific example of this idea: Biden's eulogy of McCain was found in the *Springfield News-Sun* article "Read Joe Biden's Eulogy of John McCain," by Debbie Lord, August 30, 2018.

Chapter 7: Become an Ally

172 For instance, according to Dr. Thomas Vance: Dr. Vance is quoted from his article on the website of the Columbia University Department of Psychiatry, "Addressing Mental Health in the Black Community," February 8, 2019.

173 It was not until 2020: The LGBTQ+ Supreme Court ruling was covered in the *New York Times* article "Civil Rights Law Protects Gay and Transgender Workers, Supreme Court Rules," by Adam Liptak, June 15, 2020.

173 "Stigma-related prejudice": Cathy Kelleher's work is from her *Counselling Psychology Quarterly* paper "Minority Stress and Health: Implications for Lesbian, Gay, Bisexual, Transgender, and Questioning (LGBTQ) Young People," December 14, 2009.

174 Brad Brenner, PhD: Dr. Brenner is quoted from his Anxiety and Depression Association of America article "Understanding Anxiety and Depression for LGBTQ People."

175 The Deloitte University Leadership Center: The survey was taken from the *Harvard Business Review* article "Help Your Employees Be Themselves at Work," by Dorie Clark and Christie Smith, November 3, 2014.

176 Howard Schultz, former CEO of Starbucks: Schultz was quoted in the CNN article "Former Starbucks CEO Howard Schultz: 'I Honestly Don't See Color,'" by Kate Sullivan, February 13, 2019.

176 Says activist Franchesca Ramsey: Ramsey is quoted from her *Glamour* article "How to Respond When Someone Says, 'I Don't See Color'—and Six Other Cringe-Worthy Remarks," May 21, 2018.

176 Statements denying there's a problem: Janice Gassam's citation is from her *Forbes* article "Why the 'I Don't See Color' Mantra Is Hurting Your Diversity and Inclusion Efforts," February 15, 2019.

177 Two of the leading scholars in implicit bias: Drs. Banaji and Greenwald's book is *Blindspot*, Delacorte Press (2013). Also noted in this section is information from the *Vox* article "Implicit Bias Means We're All Probably at Least a Little Bit Racist," by Jenée Desmond-Harris, August 15, 2016.

179 20 percent of large US companies today: The statistics on implicit bias training are from the College and Research Libraries News article "Minimizing and Addressing Implicit Bias in the Workplace," by Shamika Dalton and Michele Villagran, October 2018, which references the University of North Carolina Chapel Hill Executive Development paper "The Real Effects of Unconscious Bias in the Workplace," by Horace McCormick, 2016.

180 Says Katie Burke, chief people officer for HubSpot: Burke is quoted from her *Inc.* article "3 Things You Can Do Now to Take Action as an Ally in the Workplace," October 29, 2018.

181 Rosabeth Moss Kanter, professor at Harvard Business School: Dr. Kanter's quote is ubiquitous; we cite it from QuoteFancy.com.

182 One study at Marquette University: The study is quoted on the USC Center for Health Journalism website article "How Racism and Microaggressions Lead to Worse Health," by Gina Torino, November 10, 2017.

184 Karen Catlin, author of *Better Allies*: Catlin's quote is from her Medium.com column "5 Things Allies Can Do to Sponsor Coworkers from Underrepresented Groups," May 22, 2020.

185 Good allies don't hide in the shadows: Dr. Isaac Sabat is quoted from the CNN article "Sharing the Weight: How to Know When—and How—to Support Marginalized People at Work," by Julia Carpenter, October 30, 2018.

186 Susan Wojcicki, CEO of YouTube: Wojcicki is quoted from her *Vanity Fair* article "Exclusive: How to Break Up the Silicon Valley Boys Club," March 16, 2017.

Chapter 8: Transform Exclusion into Connection
189 work done at Cornell University: The firehouse data can be found in the *Cornell Chronicle* article "Groups That Eat Together Perform Better Together," by Susan Kelley, November 19, 2015.

190 FOMO and being excluded: Dr. Sandra Robinson's work is referenced on the University of British Columbia website article "Ostracism More Damaging Than Bullying in the Workplace," by Andrew Riley, May 29, 2014.

195 We had a chance to interview Mitt Romney: Romney's story is from his foreword to Adrian Gostick and Dana Telford's *The Integrity Advantage*, Gibbs Smith (2003).

199 Emma Seppälä and Marissa King of Yale: Drs. Seppälä and King are quoted in the *Inc.* article "Tom Brady Just Answered 'Yes' to a Very Controversial Question," by Bill Murphy Jr., April 26, 2020; and their *Harvard Business Review* article "Having Friends at Work Can Be Tricky, but It's Worth It," August 8, 2017.

200 the wayward wisdom of Michael Scott: The quote is from season 2, episode 6 of *The Office*, "The Fight" (2005).

202 Executive coach Peter Bregman: We spoke with Bregman and also borrowed from his *Harvard Business Review* article "How to Have Friends at Work When You're the Boss," March 19, 2014.

203 Says Professor Art Markman: Dr. Markman is quoted from his *Harvard Business Review* article "Why Work Friendships Go Awry, and How to Prevent It," June 8, 2018.

203 We turn to a commencement address: Oprah's 2013 commencement address can be read in its entirety in the *Harvard Gazette* article "Winfrey's Commencement Address," from May 30, 2013 (posted May 31, 2013).

207 Beth Schinoff of Boston College: Drs. Schinoff et al. are quoted from their *Harvard Business Review* article "How Remote Workers Make Work Friends," by Beth Schinoff, Blake E. Ashforth, and Kevin Corley, November 22, 2019.

Chapter 9: Turn Doubts into Assurance
213 Research conducted for us by Willis Towers Watson: The Willis Towers Watson data is from Adrian Gostick and Chester Elton's *The Carrot Principle*, Simon & Schuster (2009).

214 they are better able to bounce back from adversity: Dr. Algoe is quoted from her *Social and Personality Psychology Compass* paper "Find, Remind, and Bind: The Functions of Gratitude in Everyday Relationships," May 31, 2012.

216 Studies by a team of scientists: Dr. McCraty is quoted from the positive psychology.com article "The Neuroscience of Gratitude and How It Affects Anxiety and Grief," by Madhuleena Roy Chowdhury, May 5, 2020.

217 Rock star Bruce Springsteen's autobiography: *Born to Run* was published by Simon & Schuster (2016); *Born Standing Up* was put out by Scribner (2007); and Lady Gaga is quoted from her 2011 HBO concert documentary, *Lady Gaga Presents the Monster Ball Tour: At Madison Square Garden*, noted in the *InStyle* article "25 Stars Who Suffer from Imposter Syndrome," by Samantha Simon, December 8, 2017.

217 UCLA neuroscientist Dr. Alex Korb: Dr. Korb's work is found in his book *The Upward Spiral*, New Harbinger Publications (2015).

Conclusion: The Semicolon

227 Take the example of Madalyn Parker: Parker's story was in the CNN article "When a Woman Took Sick Days for Mental Health, Her Email Sparked a Larger Discussion," by Rose Schmidt, July 13, 2017.

228 Heather Parrie, a Missouri accountant: Parrie's autobiographical account can be found in her *HuffPost* article "My Semicolon Tattoo Is More Than Art. It's a Reminder to Keep Going," July 14, 2015.

About the Authors

Adrian Gostick is the author of such books as *The Carrot Principle*, *Leading with Gratitude*, and *All In*, which have been *New York Times* and *Wall Street Journal* bestsellers. His works have been translated into more than thirty languages and have sold 1.5 million copies around the world. He has appeared on NBC's *Today* show and been quoted in the *Economist*, *Financial Times*, *Harvard Business Review*, *Wall Street Journal*, and *Fortune*; and he is a leadership strategy contributor to *Forbes*. Gostick is the cofounder of the motivation assessment firm FindMojo.com. He is ranked among the top ten global gurus in leadership and is ranked the number three organizational culture expert in the world. Learn more about Adrian's writing, speaking, and executive coaching at GostickandElton.com.

Chester Elton's work is supported by research with more than one million working adults. He has been called the "apostle of appreciation" by Canada's *Globe and Mail*, "creative and refreshing" by the *New York Times*, and a "must read for modern managers" by CNN. Elton is coauthor of *The Carrot Principle*, *Leading with Gratitude*, and *All In*, and has been quoted in publications such as the *Wall Street Journal*, the *Washington Post*, and *Fast Company*. A sought-after lecturer around the world, he is ranked among the top ten global gurus in leadership and is ranked the number two organizational culture expert in the world. He is cofounder of FindMojo.com, and 700,000 people follow his work on LinkedIn. Learn more about Chester's speaking, coaching, and writing at GostickandElton.com.

Anthony Gostick earned a bachelor's degree with honors in biotechnology and has three years' experience working as a researcher and laboratory lead in NIH-funded genetics labs. He deferred offers to study genetics at the graduate level from the University of Southern California and Johns Hopkins University to help research and write this book. Anthony is passionate about raising awareness of mental health issues.

We Thrive Together

Adrian, Chester, and Anthony have created the We Thrive Together community, which brings together passionate working adults and leaders to eliminate the stigma of anxiety at work and create positive mental health in the workplace. There is no charge to join or be a member of Thrive, and the site contains a wealth of resources and peer support. Find a link to the community at GostickandElton.com.